Israel ar

Israel and Palestine

Competing Histories

Mike Berry and Greg Philo

LONDON • ANN ARBOR, MI

First published 2004. This expanded version first published 2006 by
Pluto Press
345 Archway Road, London N6 5AA
and 839 Greene Street, Ann Arbor, MI 48106

www.plutobooks.com

British Library Cataloguing in Publication Data
A catalogue record for this book is available from the British Library

Hardback
ISBN-13 978 0 7453 2566 8
ISBN-10 0 7453 2566 1

Paperback
ISBN-13 978 0 7453 2565 1
ISBN-10 0 7453 2565 3

Library of Congress Cataloging in Publication Data applied for

10 9 8 7 6 5 4 3 2 1

Designed and produced for Pluto Press by
Chase Publishing Services Ltd, Fortescue, Sidmouth, EX10 9QG, England
Typeset from disk by Stanford DTP Services, Northampton, England
Printed and bound in the European Union by
Antony Rowe Ltd, Chippenham and Eastbourne, England

Contents

MAPS

Introduction

This book was developed from work that we originally undertook for our study of TV news coverage of the Israeli/Palestinian conflict.* When we began that research we thought it would be useful to give a brief history partly because there was a great deal of public interest in the area and also because we wanted to show the complex arguments through which journalists had to pick their way when making news programmes. It quickly became apparent to us that there was not one history of the conflict but many, since almost every historical fact was contested by one or other of the parties. There were many deep divisions of opinion, not only between the Israeli and Palestinian historians but also within each side. Such divisions always to some extent characterise academic debate, but in this case there was also a strong ideological dimension, since the different interpretations and historical accounts could be used to justify and legitimise political positions. The Israeli historian Avi Shlaim has written of the 'history wars' in which the traditional Zionist account of the birth of Israel was challenged by a new group of Israeli historians who were much more critical of the role of Israel in the generation and continuation of the conflict. These historians, including Ilan Pappe and Shlaim himself, were attacked publicly in Israel. As Avi Shlaim writes of his critics:

> They would like school history books to continue to tell only the heroic version of Israel's creation. In effect they were saying that in education, one has to lie for the good of the country. (2003: 9)

What concerned the conservative critics was their belief that the new historians had undermined patriotic values and

* This was published as *Bad News from Israel* (Pluto Press, 2004).

young people's confidence in the justice of Israel's cause. Six months before the Israeli election of January 2001 Ariel Sharon commented that 'the new historians should not be taught'. When the new right-wing government came to power under Ariel Sharon in 2001 the education minister ordered changes. As Shlaim notes:

> One of the first things Ms Livnat did on becoming Minister of Education was to order new history textbooks for secondary schools to be written, removing all traces of the influence of the new historians. (2003:10)

It is clear, then, that there are many different narratives and that they are sometimes bound up in attempts to defend the moral certainties of the contending parties. In this book we have outlined the range of different positions and arguments on all the major events in the history of the conflict. However, we have not simply repeated these without comment. We are not 'post-modern' in our approach and we do not believe that all accounts should be seen as equally valid. There is a difference between those who make statements without apparent recourse to evidence and others who spend long hours in archives, researching and checking their conclusions. There will always be contestation, but as far as possible we have indicated which views are best supported by available evidence and where there are contradictions or inaccuracies in what is being said. We have, however, tried to do this with a light touch because in the end it is up to our readers to make their own decisions on the validity of accounts and on what they believe. Finally, we hope that in laying out the range of arguments in a clear and accessible fashion, we may contribute to a better-informed public debate in an area that has so often been full of propaganda and confusion.

ZIONIST ROOTS AND THE FIRST WAVE OF JEWISH IMMIGRATION INTO PALESTINE

The American historian Howard Sachar (1977) traces the contemporary emergence of Zionist thought to the European Rabbis, Judah Alkalai and Zvi Hirsh Kalischer, who from the 1830s onwards stressed the need for Jews to return to the Holy Land as a necessary prelude to the Redemption and the coming of the Messiah. Sachar argues that such messianic exhortations did not immediately or widely take root among European Jews. However, he suggests that by the 1870s societies generally known as *Chovevei Zion* ('Lovers of Zion') had formed across Russia, which viewed Palestine as a site for national renewal and a refuge from anti-Semitism.

In 1881, following the assassination of Tsar Alexander II, large numbers of Jews were killed in a series of Russian pogroms. By 1914 up to two million Jews had fled Russia to escape persecution. The vast majority sought sanctuary in the United States but 25,000 arrived in Palestine in two waves of immigration in 1882–84 and 1890–91. At the time the Jewish population in Palestine was small. The official Ottoman census of 1878 had put the total at 15,011 living among a combined Muslim/Christian population of 447,454 (McCarthy, 1990). The newcomers, backed with Jewish capital from prominent families such as the Rothschilds, saw themselves as agricultural pioneers, who were working to establish the foundations of Jewish self-determination in Palestine. A letter dated 21 September 1882 from Vladimir Dubnow, a worker at the Mikveh Israel agricultural settlement, to his brother Simon, captures the sentiments and hopes of the early Jewish settlers:

> My ultimate aim, like that of many others, is greater, broader, incomprehensible but not unattainable. The final goal is eventually to gain control of Palestine and to restore to the Jewish people the political independence of which it has been deprived for two thousand years. Don't laugh this is no illusion. The means for realising this goal is at hand: the founding of settlements in the country based on agriculture and crafts, the establishment and gradual expansion of all sorts of factories, in brief – to make an effort so that all the

land, all the industry will be in Jewish hands. In addition, it will be necessary to instruct young people and the future generation in the use of firearms (in free, wild Turkey anything can be done), and then – here I too am plunging into conjecture – then the glorious day will dawn of which Isaiah prophesised in his burning and poetic utterances. The Jews will proclaim in a loud voice and if necessary with arms in their hands that they are the masters of their ancient homeland. (cited in Gilbert, 1999: 5–6)

Relations between the new Jewish immigrants and the native population were mixed. Jewish settlements were built on land that was purchased from absentee *effendi* landlords. Often the locals who had tended the land were evicted with the help of Turkish police, and this led to resentment and violence. Some Zionists such as Ahad Aham were very critical of the way the settlers gained control of the land and treated the local population. In 1891 he argued that the settlers 'treat the Arabs with hostility and cruelty and, unscrupulously deprive them of their rights, insult them without cause and even boast of such deeds; and none opposes this despicable and dangerous inclination' (1923: 107, cited in Hirst, 1977: 24). There was also evidence that the two groups were able partially to accommodate each other because the settlers also brought benefits. They provided employment opportunities, access to medical care, the loan of modern equipment and a market for produce. Sachar reports that in the 1890s the agricultural settlement of Zichron Ya'akov employed more than a thousand Arabs working for 200 Jews. The former *Guardian* Middle East correspondent David Hirst (1977) argues that the beginning of the twentieth century saw the arrival of a more militant type of settler to Palestine, inspired by the ideas of Theodor Herzl and determined to take control of the land and exclude non-Jews from the labour market. The Jewish National Fund, set up to manage Jewish land purchases, decreed in 1901 that all land it purchased could never be resold or leased to gentiles, and settlers began to boycott Arab labour (Hirst, 1977; Shafir, 1999).

THEODOR HERZL AND THE EMERGENCE OF POLITICAL ZIONISM

Theodor Herzl, who is commonly regarded as the father of political Zionism, was a Jewish Austro-Hungarian journalist and playwright. He had been deeply affected by the virulent anti-Semitism sweeping across Europe, and as a journalist for the Vienna newspaper *Neue Freie Presse* had covered the notorious Dreyfus trial in Paris, where a Jewish officer was falsely charged with passing secrets to the Germans. He had also been alarmed by the election of Karl Lueger as mayor of Vienna at the head of an openly anti-Semitic party. Herzl felt that a central issue for Jews was their dispersal across the Diaspora and their existence as a minority in each country they inhabited. This, Herzl argued, led to a dependence on the host culture and a suppression of self-determination. Furthermore Herzl believed that widespread anti-Semitism meant that complete assimilation into European society was an impossibility for most Jews. The solution he laid out in *Der Judenstaat* or *The Jewish State* (1896) was for Jews to create their own state, in which they would constitute a majority and be able to exercise national self-determination. In contrast to the 'practical Zionism' of the Jewish settlers who began to arrive in Palestine from 1882, Herzl adopted a political orientation, cultivating links with prominent imperial statesmen in an attempt to gain a charter for Jewish land settlement.

Herzl had two potential locations in mind for the prospective Jewish state: Argentina and Palestine. His diaries show that he was greatly influenced by the British imperialist Cecil Rhodes, and in particular the manner in which Rhodes had gained control of Mashonaland and Matabeleland from its inhabitants (Hirst, 1977). In his diaries Herzl suggests that the settlers should follow Rhodes's example and 'gently' expropriate the native population's land and 'try to spirit the penniless population across the border by procuring employment for it in the transit countries, while denying it any employment in our own country', but that 'the process of expropriation and the removal of the poor must be carried out discreetly and circumspectly' (Herzl, 1960: 88, cited in Hirst, 1977: 18). In order to further this aim Herzl sought out an imperial sponsor prepared to grant a settlement charter. He canvassed Germany's Kaiser, the Ottoman Sultan and Britain's Joseph Chamberlain, stressing to each the benefits that a Jewish state and Jewish capital could bring. In 1901 Herzl travelled to Constantinople and met the Sultan. Herzl offered capital to refinance the Ottoman public debt in what turned out to be a failed attempt to gain a charter for the establishment of a Jewish Ottoman Colonisation Association in Palestine. Bohm (1935) claims that the third article of the proposed charter would have given the Jewish administration the right to deport the native population from Palestine.

Herzl subsequently switched his attention to lobbying British politicians. Hirst (1977) suggests that Herzl linked Zionist ambitions to British imperial interests, and tried to play on the anti-Semitism of certain British politicians by arguing that a Jewish homeland would lessen the flow of Jewish refugees, who were fleeing pogroms, into Britain. During this period there was a fear among some members of the British establishment that Jews were agents of Bolshevism. Herzl lobbied Lord Rothschild for the creation of Jewish colonies in Cyprus, the Sinai peninsula and Egyptian Palestine, but the plans met with resistance from the Egyptian authorities. In April 1903, Neville Chamberlain proposed to Herzl that the Zionists set up a homeland in Uganda under the sovereignty of the British crown. Chamberlain offered a territory under the control of a Jewish governor into which a million Jews could immigrate and settle (Gilbert, 1999). Herzl accepted the plan. Martin Gilbert suggests that Herzl 'was determined to take up the first offer presented to the Jews by a great power, and to provide at least a place of temporary asylum for the Jews of Russia' (1999: 21). The proposal did not receive universal endorsement from Zionists, but at the Sixth Zionist Conference in Basle in 1903 Herzl succeeded in securing a majority in favour of the Uganda scheme: 295 voted for the proposal, 175 voted against and 99 abstained. However, shortly afterwards, in July 1903, Herzl died at the age of 44 and with him the Uganda project, which was rejected by the 1904 Zionist conference.

The task of forwarding political Zionism passed to the chemist, Chaim Weizmann.

THE SECOND WAVE OF JEWISH IMMIGRATION INTO PALESTINE

1904 saw the beginning of another wave of Jewish immigration into Palestine, again as a result of Russian pogroms. Over the next ten years between 35,000 and 40,000 Jewish immigrants arrived. Among this group was a twenty-year-old Russian Jew, David Gruen (later changed to Ben-Gurion, or son of Gruen), who arrived in Jaffa in September 1906 and was later to play a pivotal role in the creation and development of the Israeli state. The new immigrants mostly worked as labourers on the agricultural settlements established by the previous wave of Jewish immigrants, or in the towns. They also established the first Jewish political parties, a Hebrew-language press, collective farms (kibbutzim) and in 1909 the first Jewish self-defence militia, Ha-Shomer (The Watchman), with the motto 'By blood and fire Judaea fell; by blood and fire Judaea shall rise' (Gilbert, 1999: 27). The Israeli sociologist Gershon Shafir argues that the struggle to create an all-Jewish labour force transformed Jewish workers into 'militant nationalists' who 'sought to establish a homogenous Jewish society' (1999: 88). Palestine became the site for two emerging and competing nationalisms: first, the native Muslim and Christian population keen to throw off Ottoman rule and, second, the Jewish newcomers determined to create their own homeland. Some Zionists began to stress the importance of armed force. Israel Zangwill, who had coined the Zionist slogan 'a land without people for a people without land', informed a meeting of Zionists in Manchester in 1905 that '[We] must be prepared either to drive out by the sword the [Arab] tribes in possession as our forefathers did or to grapple with the problem of a large alien population' (Zwangill, cited in Morris, 2001: 140).

The Palestinians, as a subject population under Ottoman rule, were initially deferential in their protests. During the 1890s members of the Palestinian elite repeatedly and unsuccessfully petitioned their imperial overlords in Constantinople to limit of Mecca, who was recognised as the Keeper of Islam's most holy places.[1] However, these pledges by European Powers to strive for the recognition of Arab independence conflicted with British assurances also given at the time to Zionist leaders, that Britain would seek the establishment of a Jewish homeland in Palestine. Zionist leaders established close links with prominent British politicians including Lloyd George, Arthur Balfour, Herbert Samuel and Mark Sykes. In 1915 Samuel, in a memorandum entitled 'The Future of Palestine', proposed 'the British annexation of Palestine [where] we might plant three or four million European Jews' (Weisgal, 1944: 131, cited in UN, 1990). British support for a Jewish homeland was made explicit in the Balfour Declaration of November 1917:

> His Majesty's Government view with favour the establishment in Palestine of a national home for the Jewish people, and will use their best endeavours to facilitate the achievement of this object, it being clearly understood that nothing shall be done which may prejudice the civil and religious rights of existing non-Jewish communities in Palestine or the rights and political status enjoyed by Jews in any other country.

The 'non-Jewish communities', which comprised the 89 per cent of the population, who were Arab, Muslim and Christian, were angered by the declaration.[2] They noted that it only spoke of their 'civil and religious rights', making no mention of political rights. They also questioned the right of the British to give away a country that did not belong to them. Conversely, for the Zionists the declaration was regarded as a triumph. The Israeli historian Avi Shlaim, paraphrasing Chaim Weizmann, argues that it 'handed the Jews a golden key to unlock the doors of Palestine and make themselves the masters of the country' (2000: 7). The legality of the Balfour Declaration has since been questioned by some experts (Linowitz, 1957; Cattan, 1973).

After the First World War Britain was assigned control of Palestine, through the mandates system governing the dismemberment of the Ottoman Empire. In 1921, the British divided the area in two, with the sector east of the Jordan

River becoming Transjordan and the area west of the river the Palestinian mandate. In July 1922, the League of Nations Council ratified the Palestinian mandate, article four of which stated that 'an appropriate Jewish agency shall be recognized as a public body for the purpose of advising and co-operating with the administration of Palestine in such economic, social and other matters as may affect the establishment of the Jewish National Home' (Gilbert, 1999: 50). For many supporters of the Israeli state the inclusion of the terms of the Balfour Declaration into the League of Nations mandate provide a legal justification for the creation of the Israeli state in Palestine. The view of Palestinians is that such agreements were essentially colonialist in nature and the Jewish presence no more legitimate than the French settler colonies in Algeria, which were evacuated after independence.

The indigenous population of mandated Palestine feared mass Jewish immigration would lead to the further colonisation of their country, and that this would be followed by their own subjugation. The view was shared by certain prominent British politicians such as Lord Curzon who, on 26 January 1919, commented to Lord Balfour:

> I feel tolerably sure therefore that while Weizmann may say one thing to you, or while you may mean one thing by a national home, he is out for something quite different. He contemplates a Jewish State, a Jewish nation, a subordinate population of Arabs, etc. ruled by Jews; the Jews in possession of the fat of the land, and directing the Administration ... He is trying to effect this behind the screen and under the shelter of British trusteeship. (British Government, Foreign Office, 1919a, cited in Ingrams, 1972: 58)

Some members of the British establishment believed that by supporting the Jewish national home they were directly violating the terms of the mandate.[3] Others seemed less concerned about the opinions of the Arab population. A senior British official was cited as telling Chaim Weizmann that in Palestine 'there are a few hundred thousand Negroes but that is a matter of no significance' (Heller, 1985, cited in Chomsky, 1992: 435). Some historians, however, have disputed the notion that the Jewish immigrants intended to dominate or supplant the native Arab population. Martin Gilbert, for instance, has claimed that the Jewish immigrants intended to develop the country for the mutual benefit of both peoples and were very concerned about the impact of Jewish immigration on the indigenous population:

> Ben-Gurion sought to combine the dynamic of Jewish settlement with the basically humane ideals of Judaism as it had evolved over the centuries. The rights of the inhabitants of the land – not always respected in biblical times – were for him of great importance. Co-existence with the Arabs would, as he saw it, benefit the Arabs considerably, without in any way dispossessing them. (1999: 38)

Other commentators such as ex-prime minister Binyamin Netanyahu have argued that the Jewish settlers had more of a right to the land than the native population because more than 2,000 years earlier Jews had lived there, and in the intervening years had never relinquished their claim over the land. Netanyahu also maintained that Jewish claims to the land were superior to those of the native population because the land had allegedly not been fully developed:

> In many ways the argument between Jews and Arabs over their respective historic rights to a national home resembles an argument over the rights of an individual owner to his house. If the original owner is tossed out of his home but never relinquishes his right to return and re-occupy his premises, he may press his claim. But suppose a new occupant has fixed up the place and made a home of it while the original claimant is still around but prevented from pressing his claim? In such a case even if the new occupant has resided there for a considerable period of time and improved the premises, his claim to the place is considered inferior to that of the original owner. Yet in the meantime no one has set up house and the place has become a shambles, there can be no rival claim, and the original owner is clearly entitled to have his property back. (Netanyahu, 2000: 27–8)

Between 1919 and 1926 the Jewish presence in Palestine swelled with the arrival of a further 90,000 immigrants

(Bregman, 2003). Gilbert claims that anti-Semitic violence in the Ukraine, in which 100,000 Jews were killed in the aftermath of the First World War, as well as increasing persecution in Poland acted as a 'powerful catalyst for immigration' (1999: 49). The Jewish community in Palestine also became increasingly militarised, with the creation of what Shlaim describes as an 'iron wall' of impregnable strength, designed to protect Jewish settlements from Arab attacks. The concept of the 'iron wall' had first been deployed by Vladimar Jabotinsky, the leader of the Revisionist movement.[4] Jabotinsky was convinced that the indigenous Arabs would not accept the Zionist project voluntarily and advocated the creation of an 'iron wall' that the local population would be unable to breach:

> If you wish to colonise a land in which people are already living, you must provide a garrison for the land, or find a benefactor who will maintain the garrison on your behalf. Zionism is a colonising adventure and therefore it stands or falls by the question of armed forces. (Jabotinsky, cited in Masalha, 1992: 45)

The Zionists also substantially increased their land holdings. Agricultural land was purchased from absentee Arab landlords. The peasants who tended and lived on it were evicted. The 1919 American King–Crane Commission, which had been sent to Palestine to assess local opinion, reported in their discussions with Jewish representatives, that 'the Zionists looked forward to a practically complete dispossession of the present non-Jewish inhabitants of Palestine, by various forms of purchase' (British Government, 1947: 3, cited in Laqueur & Rubin, 1984: 29). The Zionists also increasingly boycotted Arab labour. The British Hope-Simpson Commission had criticised the Zionist Keren ha-Yesod employment agreements as discriminatory and pointed to article seven, which stipulated that 'The settler hereby undertakes that ... if and whenever he may be obliged to hire help, he will hire Jewish workmen only', and article eleven, which stated that 'the settler undertakes ... not to hire any outside labour except Jewish labourers' (British Government, Cmd. 3686: 52–3, cited in UN, 1990). The tensions created by this labour exclusivism, the commission reported, constituted 'a constant and increasing source of danger to the country' (British Government, Cmd. 3686: 55, cited in UN, 1990).

Throughout the 1920s Arab hostility to the Zionist project manifested itself in increasingly prolonged outbreaks of violence. In 1921 Arabs attacked Jews at Jaffa during a May Day parade, and the violence spread to other towns and the countryside. By the time the British army brought the situation under control nearly 200 Jews and 120 Arabs were dead or wounded. Britain set up a commission of inquiry to investigate the violence. The Haycraft Commission reported that the violence was spontaneous and anti-Zionist rather than anti-Jewish. The report blamed the Arabs for the violence, but also pointed to Arab fears that the mass influx of Jewish immigrants would lead to their subjugation. General William Congreve, the commander of British forces in the Middle East, criticised Herbert Samuel's policy of trying to establish a Jewish national home in Palestine in the face of the opposition from most of the population (Ovendale, 1999). Shortly afterwards the Arabs sent a petition to the League of Nations asking for democratic elections and independence for Palestine (Segev, 2001). In 1922 the British government published a White Paper, which was intended to mollify Arab fears. It denied that the Balfour Declaration paved the way for a Jewish state, and that the Arab population, culture and language would be subordinated. It also proposed a legislative council made up of Jewish, Muslim and Christian representatives, a suggestion that was rejected by the Arabs. Hirst (1977) alleges that a large proportion of the council would have been directly appointed by Britain. This would have been likely to give the Jewish representatives a majority. The Palestinians therefore feared that Zionist policies might be legitimised under a constitutional façade.

The 1920s and 1930s saw more violent disturbances followed on each occasion by commissions of inquiry dispatched by Britain to examine causes. After 1921 there was a period of relative calm before the next major outbreak of violence in 1929. The flashpoint for the violence was a dispute over sovereignty of an area containing important Jewish and Muslim religious sites.

Tension had been brewing for some months over this issue, fomented by inflammatory rhetoric in the Arab and Hebrew press. In late August 1929, a group of armed Arabs attacked Jewish worshippers in Jerusalem, and in a week of rioting and violence 113 Jews and 116 Arabs were killed. In Hebron, Arab rioters killed more than 60 members of a long-standing community of non-Zionist religious Jews. In response the British set up the Shaw Commission of Inquiry, which concluded that the trigger for the violence was Jewish demonstrations at the Wailing Wall but that the underlying causes were economic and political grievances on the part of the Arabs against the mandate. It found that the effects of mass Jewish immigration had been 'to arouse among Arabs the apprehension that they will in time be deprived of their livelihood and pass under the political domination of the Jews' (cited in Gilbert, 1999: 64). An Arab delegation including the Mufti of Jerusalem met British officials in London requesting a prohibition on the sale of lands from Arabs to non-Arabs, an end to Jewish immigration and the formation of a national parliament.

The Hope-Simpson Commission dispatched by Britain shortly afterwards highlighted the problem of a growing population of landless Arabs and recommended controls on Jewish immigration and land purchase. These recommendations were carried through in the 1930 Passfield White Paper. However, these developments were regarded as a serious setback by Zionists who managed through lobbying to reverse the terms of the White Paper. Gilbert suggests that there were two reasons the Zionists were strongly opposed to the recommendations of the commission: first, they wanted to keep open Palestine as a site for mass immigration, especially in view of the increased persecution of Jews throughout Europe and, second, they feared that without mass immigration they would remain a minority within Palestine subject to the control of the Arab majority. He cites a letter dated 3 December 1931 from Arthur Ruppin, a prominent Zionist, which captures this sentiment:

At most, the Arabs would agree to grant national rights to the Jews in an Arab state, on the pattern of national rights in Eastern Europe. But we know

> only too well from conditions in Eastern Europe how little a majority with executive power can be moved to grant real and complete national equality to a minority. The fate of the Jewish minority in Palestine would always be dependent upon the goodwill of the Arab majority, which would steer the state. (cited in Gilbert, 1999: 66)

Sporadic violence ignited into a full-scale Arab rebellion in the years between 1936 and 1939. Part of the revolt involved peaceful resistance, including a nationwide six-month strike and widespread non-payment of taxes. It also involved extensive violence in which Palestinians formed into bands and destroyed crops and trees, mined roads and sabotaged infrastructure and oil pipelines. They attacked and killed Jews, and also targeted Arabs who failed to offer support or who were suspected of collaboration. Gilbert claims that during this period 'most acts of Arab terror were met, often within a few hours, by equally savage acts of reprisal by the Revisionists' military arm, the Irgun' (1999: 92). The Arabs demanded democratic elections and an end to immigration. The British dispatched another commission of inquiry, which in 1937 stated that the mandate was unworkable and recommended partition. The Peel Commission proposed that the north-west part of Palestine, accounting for 20 per cent of the country though containing its most fertile land, would become a Jewish state, while the remaining 80 per cent would become an Arab state linked to Transjordan. A corridor to the sea would remain under British control, as would Jerusalem and Bethlehem.

The proposal received a mixed reception among Jews. One group, centred on Jabotinsky's Revisionists, argued that a Jewish state should only be set up in the whole of Palestine and Transjordan. Another, which included Weizmann and David Ben-Gurion, argued that this was a historic opportunity to create the Jewish state. The Israeli historian Simha Flapan suggests that Ben-Gurion accepted the plan as a stepping stone to Zionist control of all of Palestine, and points to comments he made before the Zionist executive in 1937 that: 'after the formation of a large army in the wake of the establishment of the [Jewish] state, we shall abolish partition and expand to

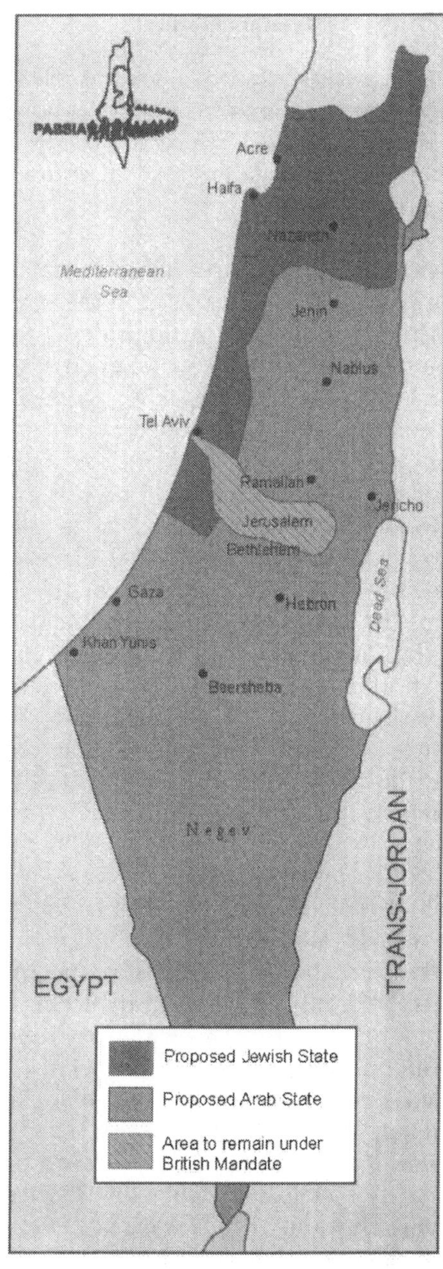

Map 1 Peel Partition Plan, 1937

the whole of the Palestine' (Ben-Gurion, cited in Flapan, 1987: 22). The Israeli historian and *Ha'aretz* columnist Tom Segev (2001) suggests that for Ben-Gurion the proposal (inherent in the Peel recommendations) for the 'forced transfer' of the Arab inhabitants out of the proposed Jewish state, and the creation therefore of a 'really Jewish' state, outweighed all the drawbacks of the proposal.

The partition plan was eventually put before the Twentieth Zionist Congress, convening in Zurich, which approved it by 299 votes to 160. The Arabs categorically rejected the partition scheme, arguing that all of Palestine was part of the Arabian homeland and it should not be broken up. The partition plans were never carried through and the rebellion continued until the British finally quelled it. The rudimentary weapons of the Arab guerrillas were overwhelmed by vastly superior British military power. Hirst (1977) claims that during this period British forces took part in extensive acts of revenge and 'collective punishment'. British soldiers descended on Arab villages, undertook summary executions and destroyed possessions and dwellings. Segev (2001) claims that torture was also employed by the British authorities. The rebellion had cost the lives of 101 Britons and 463 Jews (*The Times*, 21 July 1938, cited in Hirst, 1977: 93). Palestinian losses were harder to gauge, but Palestinian historian Walid Khalidi estimates upwards of 5,000 killed and approximately 14,000 injured (Hirst, 1977).

The reasons for these increasingly serious outbreaks of hostility between the communities are contested. Some Israelis argue that the Zionist project was essentially beneficial to the Arabs of Palestine, and it was only Arab intransigence and xenophobia that prevented mutual accommodation. Cohn-Sherbok (2001), for instance, stresses the legal basis for settlement in the Balfour Declaration, which was incorporated into the mandate, and points to the Arab rejection of partition in 1937. He argues that Arab violence directed against the Jews was 'incomprehensible' and that the Arabs were never prepared to compromise:

Throughout this period the Arab community was unwilling to negotiate over any of the issues facing those living in the Holy Land. Jews, on the other hand, continually sought to find a solution to the problems confronting the native population while retaining their conviction that a Jewish national home must be established. (Cohn-Sherbok, 2001: 179)

Martin Gilbert also argues in this vein, maintaining that 'the efforts of the Zionist leaders to come to some agreement with the Arabs of Palestine during the early 1930s were continuous'. He claims that the 'most important' of these occurred on 18 July 1934 when Ben-Gurion met Auni Abdul Hadi, the leader of the Palestinian independence movement. He cites comments made to Hadi by Ben-Gurion:

Our ultimate goal is the independence of the Jewish people in Palestine, on both sides of the Jordan, not as a minority but as a community of several millions. In my opinion, it is possible to create over a period of forty years, if Transjordan was included, a community of four million Jews in addition to an Arab community of two million ... The Arabs of Palestine would remain where they were, their lot would improve, and even politically they would not be dependent on us, even after we came to constitute the vast majority of the population. (Gilbert, 1999: 74)

Similarly, Sachar (1977) argues that the Zionist enterprise developed the country, improved the material living standards of the Arab population and provided employment opportunities. The attacks on Jews, Sachar argues, were the result of incitement by allegedly xenophobic leaders such as the Mufti of Jerusalem and agitation by fascist infiltration from Italy and Germany. Joan Peters (1984) has claimed that the Zionist project was so beneficial to the Arab population that large numbers were drawn in from outside Palestine. She attributes the large rise in the Arab population during the Mandatory period to illegal immigration from other Arab countries and argues that because of this the Jewish population in 1948 had as least as much right to the land as the Arab 'newcomers'. However, a number of British and Israeli reviewers have denounced Peters's thesis as dishonest, and most demographers attribute the bulk of the

Arab population rise to decreased mortality rates, resulting from improvements in sanitation and infrastructure.[5] Others provide different explanations for the revolt. Hirst points to economic resentment generated by peasant land evictions and the boycott of Arab labour:

> Driven from the land the peasants flocked to the rapidly growing cities in search of work. Many of them ended up as labourers building houses for the immigrants they loathed and feared. They lived in squalor. In old Haifa there were 11,000 crammed into hovels built of petrol-tins, which had neither water-supply nor rudimentary sanitation. Others, without families, slept in the open. Such conditions contrasted humiliatingly with the handsome dwellings the peasants were putting up for the well-to-do newcomers, or even with the Jewish working men's quarters furnished by Jewish building societies. They earned half or just a quarter the wage of their Jewish counterparts and Hebrew Labour exclusivism was gradually depriving them of even that. (1977: 75)

Some Israeli academics including Gershon Shafir (1999) have characterised twentieth-century Zionist settlement as similar to a form of European colonialism – the 'pure settlement colony' model, which was imposed on societies in North America and Australia. This model 'established an economy based on white labour which together with the forced removal or the destruction of the native population allowed the settlers to regain the sense of cultural and ethnic homogeneity that is identified with a European concept of nationality' (Shafir, 1999: 84). Segev argues that '"disappearing" the Arabs lay at the heart of the Zionist dream and was also a necessary condition of its realization' (2001: 405). Segev also maintains, in direct contrast with Gilbert, that prominent Zionists such as David Ben-Gurion believed that the Arab revolt was a nationalist struggle designed to prevent their dispossession:

> The rebellion cast the Arabs in a new light. Instead of a 'wild and fractured mob, aspiring to robbery and looting,' Ben-Gurion said, 'they emerged as an organized and disciplined community, demonstrating its national will with political maturity and a capacity for self-evaluation.' Were he an Arab he

wrote, he would also rebel, with even greater intensity and with greater bitterness and despair. Few Zionists understood the Arab feeling, and Ben-Gurion found it necessary to warn them: the rebellion was not just terror, he said; terror was a means to an end. Nor was it just politics, Nashashibi against the Mufti. The Arabs had launched a national war. They were battling the expropriation of their homeland. While their movement may have been primitive, Ben-Gurion said, it did not lack devotion, idealism and self-sacrifice. (Segev, 2001: 370–1)

In the wake of the revolt the British dispatched a further commission of inquiry, the result of which was the 1939 MacDonald White Paper. This proposed that 75,000 Jewish immigrants, plus 25,000 emergency refugees, be admitted over the next five years, after which any further immigration would require Arab consent.[6] The White Paper also proposed that land sales be strictly regulated and that an independent Palestine state should come about within ten years. The Zionists saw the White Paper as a betrayal, which seriously threatened the creation of a Jewish majority state in Palestine, especially in the light of the increased persecution of Jews throughout Europe. Some Israelis, including Binyamin Netanyahu, have argued that by failing to allow unrestricted Jewish immigration into Palestine, Britain was complicit in the Nazi genocide:

The extent of the British betrayal of the Jews can be understood only in the context of what was happening in Europe in the 1930s and thereafter. Responding to pressures from the Arabs, the British restriction of Jewish immigration (there was no analogous restriction on Arab immigration) cut off the routes of escape for Jews trying to flee a burning Europe. Thus, while Gestapo was conniving to send boatloads of German Jews out onto the high seas to prove that no country wanted them any more than Germany did, the British dutifully turned back every leaking barge that reached Palestine, even firing on several ... For over ten years the British shut the doors of the Jewish National Home to Jews fleeing their deaths. In doing so they not only worked to destroy the Jewish National Home, which no one believed could survive without immigrants, but made themselves accomplices in the destruction of European Jewry. (2000: 75–6)

The Jewish response to the 1939 MacDonald W[illegible] was three-pronged. One element involved maintaini[illegible] of illegal Jewish immigration into Palestine. Anothe[illegible] [illegible]ich gathered pace from 1945, saw Zionist paramilitary groups launch attacks on the British using sabotage, bombings and assassinations. The third involved switching imperial sponsors from Britain to the United States. Zionists forged close links with American political leaders and used the Jewish vote to pressurise for policies that supported the continuation of immigration and the establishment of the Jewish state in Palestine.

AMERICAN POLITICS AND THE SETTLEMENT OF THE HOLOCAUST SURVIVORS

In May 1942, Zionists meeting in New York for the American Zionist Conference issued the Biltmore Resolution, demanding the creation of a 'Jewish commonwealth' in the whole of Palestine, and began to pressurise American political leaders to support its terms. In 1941, Zionists had formed the American Palestine Committee. This included within its membership two-thirds of the Senate, 200 members of the House of Representatives and the leaders of the two main political parties and labour organisations (Ovendale, 1999). Unsuccessful resolutions were put before the House of Representatives and the Senate demanding free Jewish entry into Palestine and its reconstitution as a Jewish commonwealth. Zionist representatives also directly lobbied the two major political parties. The 1944 presidential election was a very close contest and because of this, Ovendale (1999) suggests, Zionist political leverage was considerable. America's 4,500,000 Jews were concentrated in three key states (New York, Pennsylvania and Illinois), which could swing the election. The Republican Party adopted a platform calling for unrestricted Jewish immigration into Palestine, no restrictions on land ownership and the conversion of Palestine into a free and independent Jewish commonwealth. Roosevelt was under pressure to match this, and in a private letter to Zionist leaders promised if re-elected to seek the 'establishment of Palestine as a free and democratic Jewish commonwealth' (Ovendale, 1999: 87).

The politics surrounding the settlement of Jewish refugees at the end of the Second World War are still highly contentious. The debate concerns whether the Holocaust survivors wished to settle in Palestine voluntarily, or were influenced by Zionist propaganda and left with little option. The reason for this, it is suggested, is because other potential refuges such as the United States were closed to them, and that this was with at least the tacit support of Zionist leaders. The debate remains emotive because tens of thousands of Holocaust survivors died in displaced persons (DP) camps in Europe at the end of the war. At the same time US congressional legislation gave priority to accepting refugees from the Russian-occupied states, but these included many Nazi sympathisers and ex-SS soldiers (Chomsky, 1999). Zionist leaders stressed the vital importance of Palestine as a sanctuary for the Jewish refugees in Europe who had survived the Nazi Holocaust. It was argued that only Palestine could provide a haven where Jewish refugees could rebuild their lives and avoid future anti-Semitism:

> They (the Holocaust survivors) want to regain their human dignity, their homeland, they want a reunion with their kin in Palestine after having lost their dearest relations. To them the countries of their birth are a graveyard of their people. They do not wish to return and they cannot. They want to go back to their national home, and they use Dunkirk boats. (Ben-Gurion, cited in Gilbert, 1999: 147)

Gilbert (1999) points to attempts by Holocaust survivors aboard ships such as the *Exodus* to reach Palestine as proof that most of the refugees were desperate to get there, and estimates that 40,000 Jews made their way to Palestine clandestinely between August 1945 and May 1948. Gilbert also cites comments from the British Labour MP Richard Crossman, a strong supporter of Zionism, regarding the true wishes of the Jewish refugees languishing in the DP camps who he claimed were not merely being swayed by Zionist propaganda:

> Even if there had not been a single foreign Zionist or a trace of Zionist propaganda in the camps these people would have opted for Palestine … For nine months, huddled together, these Jews had had nothing to do but discuss the future. They knew that they were not wanted by the Western democracies, and they had heard Mr Atlee's plan that they should stay and help rebuild their countries. This sounded to them pure hypocrisy. They were not Poles any more; but, as Hitler had taught them, members of the Jewish nation, despised and rejected by 'civilized Europe'. They knew that far away in Palestine there was a National Home willing and eager to receive them and to give them a chance of rebuilding their lives, not as aliens in a foreign state but as Hebrews in their own country. How absurd to attribute their longing for Palestine to organized propaganda! Judged by sober realities, their only hope of any early release was Palestine. (cited in Gilbert, 1999: 128)

The Israeli historian Yehuda Bauer (1970) also argues that most refugees were keen to settle in Palestine, citing a 1946 Hebrew investigative commission that reported that 96.8 per cent of Jewish refugees languishing in European displaced persons camps at the end of the war wanted to do so. Avi Shlaim argues that 'few people disputed the right of the Jews to a home after the trauma' of the Holocaust and that the moral case for it became 'unassailable' (2000: 23–4). But other Israeli historians suggest a different picture. Segev argues that:

> There is … no basis for the frequent assertion that the state was established as a result of the Holocaust. Clearly the shock, horror and sense of guilt felt by many generated profound sympathy for the Jews in general and the Zionist movement in particular. The sympathy helped the Zionists advance their diplomatic campaign and their propaganda, and shaped their strategy to focus effort on the survivors, those Jews in displaced-persons camps demanding they be sent to Palestine. All the survivors were Zionists, the Jewish Agency claimed, and they all wanted to come to Palestine. The assertion was not true. The displaced were given the choice of returning to their homes in Eastern Europe or settling in Palestine. Few were able or willing to return to countries then in the grip of various degrees of hunger, anti-Semitism or communism, and they were never given the option of choosing between Palestine and, say the United States. In effect their options were narrowed to Palestine or the DP camps. (2001: 491)

Others such as Feingold (1970) and Shonfeld (1977) have been highly critical of the conduct of the Zionist movement in Palestine and America at the end of the Second World War. They argue that the Zionist movement should have mobilised to pressurise the US administration to take in the Holocaust survivors, which would have saved the lives of many Jews who died in displaced persons camps in Europe. Segev argues that the Ben-Gurion and the Labour leadership in Palestine saw the Nazi ascension in the 1930s as potentially 'a fertile force for Zionism' because it created the potential for mass Jewish immigration into Palestine (1993: 18). He alleges that during the 1930s and 1940s the Labour leadership entered into *haavara* (transporting) agreements with the Nazis whereby Jews were permitted to emigrate to Palestine with limited quantities of capital. He claims that Ben-Gurion's political rivals in the Revisionist movement opposed these agreements, and argued that rather than negotiate with Germany it should be boycotted. Segev also suggests that after the *Kristallnacht* pogroms Ben-Gurion was concerned that the 'human conscience' might cause other countries to open their doors to Jewish refugees, a move that he saw as a threat to Zionism:

> If I knew that it was possible to save all the children of Germany by transporting them to England, but only half of them by transporting them to Palestine, I would choose the second – because we face not only the reckoning of those children, but the historical reckoning of the Jewish people. (Ben-Gurion, cited in Segev, 1993: 28)

The view that Jewish refugees were used as political leverage to create the Jewish state in Palestine was also shared by some prominent British and US State Department officials,[7] who feared the effects on stability in Palestine and potential Russian penetration.[8] Roosevelt's successor, Harry Truman, decided to press on with a policy supporting the settlement of Jewish refugees in Palestine. Ovendale (1999) suggests that this was primarily because of the 1945 New York election, in which the Jewish vote might be decisive. The American State Department official William Eddy claims that Truman had informed American ambassadors to the Arab world that 'I am sorry, gentlemen, but I have to answer to hundreds of thousands who are anxious for the success of Zionism; I do not have hundreds of thousands of Arabs among my constituents' (1954: 36).

THE END OF THE MANDATE

In Palestine, Zionist paramilitary groups were gradually wearing down British morale. Towards the end of the Arab revolt Jewish groups had launched attacks against the Arabs. In July 1938 more than a hundred Arabs were killed when six bombs were planted in Arab public places. The last of these, detonated in the Arab Melon market in Haifa, killed 53 Arabs and a Jew (*Palestine Post*, 26 July 1938). After the publication of the 1939 White Paper, Zionist paramilitary groups commenced operations against the British authorities. However, the outbreak of the Second World War saw the main Zionist paramilitary group, the Irgun, call off the revolt, precipitating a split within the organisation. The more militant splinter group, the Stern Gang, continued operations against the British. Following the end of the Second World War, in October 1945, the Zionist paramilitaries joined forces with the main Zionist fighting force, the Haganah, in attacking the British authorities in what became known as the 'movement of the Hebrew revolt'. Roads, bridges, trains and patrol boats were destroyed. British army barracks were attacked and banks and armouries were looted. On a single day in 1946 Zionist forces launched sixteen separate attacks on the British army, destroying many armoured vehicles and leaving 80 dead and wounded (Hirst, 1977). Lord Moyne was assassinated by the Stern Gang, British officers were captured, flogged and killed, and in the most well-known attack of all, the centre of British mandatory power in Palestine, the King David Hotel, was destroyed by 500 pounds of explosives, leaving 88 dead including 15 Jews. Funding for the attacks was provided by sympathetic sources in the United States. The Hollywood scriptwriter Ben Hecht produced an article for the *New York Herald Tribune* entitled 'Letter to the Terrorists of Palestine' in which he wrote:

> every time you blow up a British arsenal, or wreck a British jail, or send a British railway train sky high, or rob a British bank, or let go with your guns and bombs at the British betrayers and invaders of your homeland, the Jews of America make a little holiday in their hearts ... Brave friends we are working to help you. We are raising funds for you. (15 May 1947, cited in Hirst, 1977: 119)

The violence became so widespread that by early 1947 all non-essential British civilians and military families were evacuated from Palestine. Weakened by the Second World War, and demoralised by the attritional warfare, the British were rapidly losing their enthusiasm for maintaining order in Palestine. Gilbert (1999) suggests they were also wary of alienating Arab opinion because they were concerned to protect their oil interests in the region. The foreign secretary, Ernest Bevin, perhaps with this in mind, indicted that he favoured 'an independent unitary State in Palestine, with special rights for the Jewish minority, but incorporating as much as possible of the Arab plan' (cited in Gilbert, 1999: 142). Bevin also argued that a Zionist government in Palestine would be unlikely to accept any partition as final but would sooner or later seek to expand its borders. Arab hostility to the Zionist project, he predicted, might lead to long-term instability in the region: 'If Jewish irredentism is likely to develop after an interval, Arab irredentism is certain from the outset. Thus the existence of a Jewish State might prove a constant factor of unrest in the Middle East' (cited in Gilbert, 1999: 142). In February 1947 the British decided to end the mandate and hand the question of Palestine to the United Nations.

THE UNITED NATIONS DEBATES THE FUTURE OF PALESTINE

The UN dispatched a Special Committee to the region, which then recommended partition. Attention then switched to the diplomatic manoeuvring at the United Nations in New York.

Arab representatives, called before the UN, questioned whether the mandate was ever legal and whether the UN had the legal right to decide on the sovereignty of Palestine. They wished to see the issue referred to the International Court of Justice, and ultimately they argued it was the people of Palestine who should decide on the fate of the country rather than an outside body.[9] The Iraqi representative, Dr Fadhil Jamail, argued that Palestinians should not 'suffer for the crimes of Hitler' (cited in Gilbert, 1999: 144). Zionist representatives were more sympathetic to the partition plan being debated by member states and lobbied to maximise the area that might be allotted to a Jewish state. On 29 November 1947 the partition plan secured the required two-thirds majority after a last-minute change of policy by several nations,[10] with a number complaining at the political and economic pressure that had been exerted on them.[11] The Arab states as well as a number of others indicated that they did not consider themselves bound by the resolution as they argued it violated the terms of the UN Charter (United Nations, 1990). Some representatives argued that partition could create further strife and instability. The Pakistani representative, Sir Choudhri Mohammed Zafrullah Khan, stated that 'we much fear that the beneficence, if any, to which partition may lead will be small in comparison to the mischief it might inaugurate' (United Nations, 1990). Resolution 181 recommended the division of Palestine, with the Jewish state allotted 5,700 square miles including the fertile coastal areas, while the Arab state was allotted 4,300 square miles comprised mostly of the hilly areas. The proposed settlement would mean that each state would have a majority of its own population, although many Jews would fall into the Arab state and vice versa. The proposed Jewish state would, for instance, contain 500,000 Jews and 400,000 Arabs. Jerusalem and Bethlehem were to come under UN control.

For the Arabs the partition plan was a major blow. They believed that it was unfair that the Jewish immigrants, most of whom had been in Palestine less than thirty years, and who owned less than 10 per cent of the land, should be given more than half of Palestine including the best arable land. The

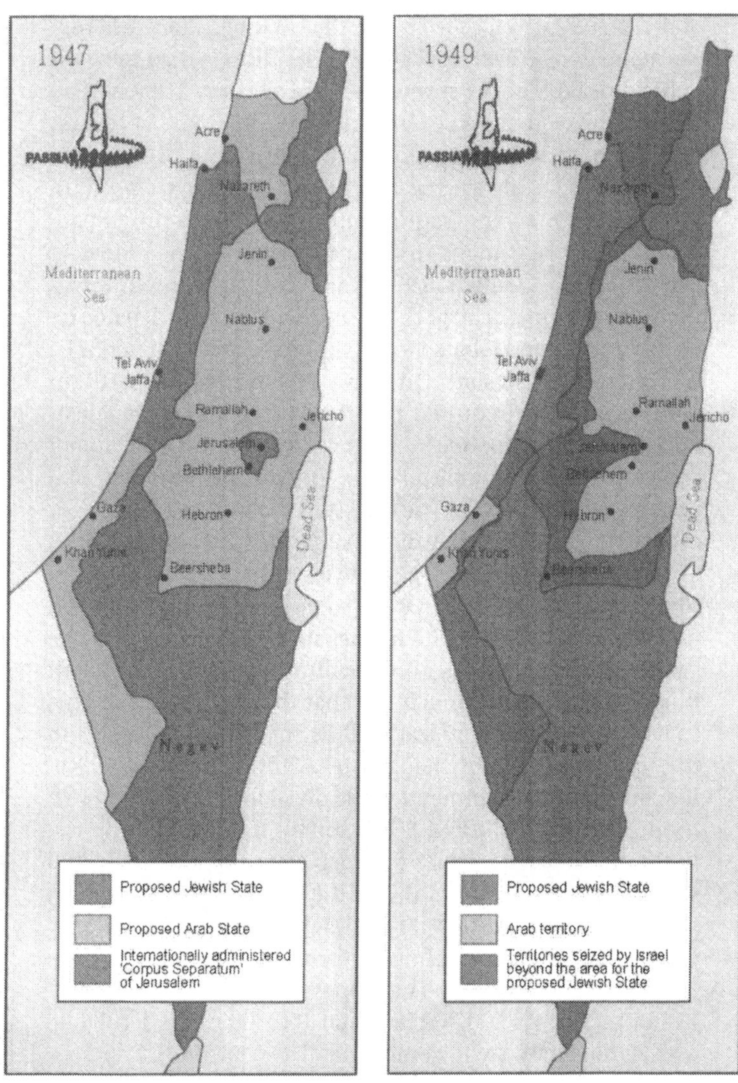

Map 2 United Nations Partition Plan, 1947 and 1949

response among many ordinary Jews in Palestine and across the Diaspora was one of celebration and jubilation. The reaction of the Zionist leadership is more contested. Some historians, such as Bregman (2003), argue that the partition resolution was seen as a triumph because it allowed for the creation of a Jewish state in an area three times that recommended by the Peel plan ten years earlier. Shlaim claims that the reaction was more ambivalent. He suggests that it was accepted by most Zionist leaders with a 'heavy heart' because they 'did not like the idea of an independent Palestinian state, they were disappointed with the exclusion of Jerusalem, and they had grave doubts about the viability of the State within the UN borders' (2000: 25). He notes that it was dismissed out of hand by Jewish paramilitary groups, who demanded all of Palestine for the Jewish state. Gilbert suggests that the Zionist leadership realised that war was inevitable and that Ben-Gurion 'contemplated the possibility of fighting to extend the area allotted to the Jews' (1999: 149). Gilbert cites orders from Ben-Gurion that Jewish forces should 'safeguard the entire Yishuv [Jewish community in Palestine] and settlements (wherever they may be), to conquer the whole country or most of it, and to maintain its occupation until the attainment of an authoritative political settlement' (Ben-Gurion, cited in Gilbert, 1999: 149). Hirst (1977) suggests that the partition plan was accepted by the Zionists because they anticipated they would quickly be able militarily to overwhelm the Arabs, and unilaterally expand the borders of the Jewish state.

This position on the relative balance of forces is contested by Netanyahu, who argues that after the partition vote the 'consensus in the governing circles of the West, friendly and unfriendly alike, was that the pinhead-sized [Jewish] state would instantly be overrun by the Arabs, and Western military strategists concurred' (2000: 83–4). But Hirst points to comments made at the time by the commander of British forces in Palestine, General J.C. Darcy, who stated that 'if you were to withdraw British troops, the Haganah [Jewish fighting forces] would take over all Palestine tomorrow' and 'could hold it against the entire Arab world' (Crum, 1947: 220, cited in Hirst, 1977: 134).

THE UNOFFICIAL WAR

The UN partition plan did not solve the problems in Palestine. The Arab Higher Committee rejected it outright and called a three-day strike. The Mufti of Jerusalem announced a jihad or struggle for Jerusalem. Fighting between the two communities broke out in early December 1947, and the situation quickly deteriorated into a civil war in which both sides attacked civilian as well as military targets (Gilbert, 1999). The British, unwilling and unable to restore order, announced they would terminate the mandate on 15 May 1948. In the first stage of the conflict lasting up to Israel's declaration of Independence on 14 May 1948, Jewish forces fought against Arab forces marshalled by three commanders: Fawzi el-Qawuqji led the Arab Liberation Army (backed by the Arab League, an organisation representing the Arab states); Sir John Bagot Glubb and his 45 British officers the Transjordian Arab Legion; and Abdul Qader al-Husseini the Mufti's Arab forces in Jerusalem (Bregman, 2003). In the early part of this 'unofficial war' the Arab forces won some minor victories and for a time al-Husseini's forces cut the road between Jerusalem and Tel-Aviv. In early April, Zionist forces launched a major offensive code named Plan Dalet. According to Avi Shlaim, the aim of Plan Dalet was 'to secure all the areas allocated to the Israeli state under the UN partition resolution as well as Jewish settlements outside these areas and corridors leading to them' (2000: 31). Arab towns and cities were captured and their populations removed so as 'to clear the interior of the country of hostile and potentially hostile Arab elements' in anticipation of an attack by the combined armies of the neighbouring Arab states (2000: 31). Shlaim notes that the Zionist offensive led to the disintegration of Palestinian society:

> The novelty and audacity of this plan lay in the order to capture Arab villages and cities, something [they] had never attempted before ... Palestinian

society disintegrated under the impact of the Jewish military offen… got underway in April, and the exodus of the Palestinians was set in motion ... by ordering the capture of Arab cities and the destruction of cities, it both permitted and justified the forcible expulsion of Arab civilians. (Shlaim, 2000: 30)

The operation involved the application of military and psychological pressure on the Arab population, who were reluctant to leave their homes. The Haganah together with paramilitary forces sprang surprise attacks on towns and villages, launching rockets, mortars and the Davidka, a device that lobbed 60 pounds of TNT 300 yards into densely populated areas (Hirst, 1977). Psychological pressure was also exerted by spreading rumours via clandestine Zionist radio stations and loudspeakers mounted on army vehicles, that Jewish forces were planning to burn villages and kill Arabs. An Israeli reserve officer recounts that:

An uncontrolled panic spread through all the Arab quarters, the Israelis brought up jeeps with loudspeakers which broadcast recorded 'horror sounds'. These included shrieks, wails and the anguished moans of Arab women, the wail of sirens and the clang of fire-alarm bells, interrupted by a sepulchral voice crying out in Arabic: 'Save your souls, all ye faithful: The Jews are using poison gas and atomic weapons. Run for your lives in the name of Allah.' (Childers, 1976: 252, cited in Hirst, 1977: 141)

In April and early May 1948, a number of Arab towns and cities fell before the Zionist offensive, creating many refugees. The aims of Plan Dalet remain highly contested among historians. Some, including Ilan Pappe, Norman Finkelstein, Nur Masalha, Walid Khalidi and David Hirst, place the operation in the context of long-held Zionist plans to 'transfer' the native population out of Palestine.[12] They argue that the notion of transfer had been inherent in Theodore Herzl's plans for Palestine some fifty years earlier (see p. 3) and had remained an integral element of Labor and Revisionist strategy. Proponents of this perspective also point to the writings of Joseph Weitz, who was appointed by the Jewish Agency to head 'transfer committees', which by the prophets of Israel; would uphold the full social and political equality of all its citizens, without distinction of religion, race or sex; and would loyally uphold the principles of the UN charter' (Shlaim, 2000: 33). The declaration did not specify the borders of the new state, because Ben-Gurion wanted to keep open the possibility of expansion beyond the UN borders. Eleven minutes later, despite objections from the State Department and US diplomatic staff, America became the first country to recognise the new Israeli state, followed soon afterwards by the Soviet Union. The following day the armies of five Arab nations, Egypt, Transjordan, Syria, Lebanon and Iraq, entered Palestine and engaged Israeli forces.

The motives of the various Arab armies and the military balance of power between Jewish and Arab forces are contested. The former head of Israeli military intelligence, Yehoshafat Harkabi, has argued that the combined Arab attack on the newly formed Israeli state essentially had two aims: to destroy the Israeli political entity (what Harkabi describes as 'politicide'), and to commit genocide against the Jewish population. Netanyahu (2000) suggests that both alleged aims were likely because the Israeli forces were outmanned and outgunned by the Arab armies:

> The common belief was that it was only a matter of time before the Jewish state, hardly in its infancy, would be terminated. Israel was coming into its War of Independence with severe handicaps imposed on it by the British ... The result was that Israel's ragtag forces were overwhelmingly outnumbered and outgunned, possessing virtually no tanks, no artillery, and no planes. As the Arab armies invaded, Israel's life hung in the balance. (2000: 84)

Other historians including Avi Shlaim have questioned these assumptions. He argues that Israeli forces actually outnumbered the Arab forces during all stages of the conflict, primarily because the five Arab nations only sent expeditionary forces, leaving the bulk of their armies at home:

> In mid-May 1948 the total number of Arab troops, both regular and irregular, operating in the Palestine theater was under 25,000, whereas

the Israel Defense Force (IDF) fielded over 35,000 troops. By mid-July the IDF mobilized 65,000 men under arms, and by December its numbers had reached a peak of 96,441. The Arab states also reinforced their armies, but they could not match this rate of increase. Thus, at each stage of the war, the IDF outnumbered all the Arab forces arrayed against it, and, after the first round of fighting, it outgunned them too. The final outcome of the war was therefore not a miracle but a faithful reflection of the underlying military balance in the Palestine theater. In this war, as in most wars, the stronger side prevailed. (Shlaim, 2005)

The picture of a monolithic Arab force determined to destroy Israel is also contested. Flapan (1987) suggests that the primary objective of King Abdullah of Transjordan (who had nominal control of all the Arab forces) was not to prevent the emergence of a Jewish state but simply to take the Arab part of Palestine, as part of a secret pact that he had made with the future Israeli prime minister Golda Meir in November 1947. Five days before the invasion of the Arab armies, on 10 May 1948, Meir had made a second secret visit to Abdullah in Amman. Alarmed that Abdullah might be backtracking on his commitment to allow the emergence of a Jewish state in exchange for annexing the Arab part of Palestine, Meir sought reassurances. However, the huge number of Palestinian refugees flooding into Transjordan as a result of Plan Dalet had created enormous popular pressure for the Arab states to intervene and halt the Jewish offensive, and Abdullah informed Meir that the situation had changed and he would be unable to keep out of the conflict. Shlaim suggests that Abdullah was dragged reluctantly into engaging by circumstances beyond his control, but nevertheless his overarching aim remained the capture of the Arab part of Palestine rather than the destruction of the Israeli state:

His objective in ordering his army across the River Jordan was not to prevent the establishment of a Jewish state but to make himself master of the Arab part of Palestine. Abdullah never wanted the other Arab armies to intervene in Palestine. Their plan was to prevent partition; his plan was to effect partition. His plan assumed and even required a Jewish presence in Palestine although his preference was for Jewish autonomy under his crown. By concentrating his forces on the West Bank, 'Abdullah intended to eliminate once and for all any possibility of an independent Palestinian state and to present his Arab partners with annexation as a *fait accompli*'. (2005)

Ovendale (1999) further suggests that the other Arab states involved were riven by competing territorial and political ambitions, in contrast to the Jewish forces, which mostly fought with a united front, and this was a decisive factor in their comprehensive defeat.[14]

In the first stage of fighting, the armies of Syria, Lebanon and Iraq made initial territorial gains, though almost all the fighting was conducted inside the area of Palestine that had been allocated by the UN to the Arab state. However, despite a serious shortage of armaments, the Israeli forces managed to quickly reverse the early Arab gains, and consolidated their hold on a number of mixed Arab-Jewish towns, eastern and western Galilee and parts of the Negev. Although Jerusalem saw very fierce fighting between Israeli and Transjordanian forces, with many casualties, Ben-Gurion was soon contemplating an offensive that would deal a decisive blow to much of the Arab coalition. On 24 May, less than ten days after Israel's Declaration of Independence, he asked the Army General Staff to prepare a plan to go on the offensive. In his war diary he wrote:

The weak link in the Arab coalition is Lebanon. Muslim rule is artificial and easy to undermine. A Christian state should be established whose southern border would be the Litani. We shall sign a treaty with it. By breaking the power of the Legion and bombing Amman, we shall also finish off Transjordan and then Syria will fall. If Egypt still dares to fight – we shall bomb Port Said, Alexandria and Cairo. (cited in Shlaim, 2005)

Such plans proved over-optimistic, however, and by the first week of June a military stalemate had ensued on all fronts. The first truce declared on 11 June came as a relief to the Israeli forces who had been heavily stretched. It also allowed the Israelis to train new recruits and arrange large shipments of armaments from Czechoslovakia in contravention of the UN arms embargo. The Arab armies did not take the opportunity to prepare themselves for another round of fighting by rearming or reorganising their forces.

During the first truce the UN appointed a mediator, the Swedish Count Bernadotte, who put forward a proposal for ending the conflict. This involved the creation of two states, one Jewish and one Arab. The Arab state would be linked politically to Transjordan, and would contain Jerusalem. Although Abdullah was keen to end hostilities the other members of the Arab League together with Israel rejected the UN plan. Bernadotte then proposed extending the truce, but this again was rejected by the Arab League with the exception of Transjordan. King Abdullah summoned Bernadotte to a meeting in Amman to express his worry that a further round of fighting could break out and recommended that the UN do all it could to prevent this. However, his efforts were undermined by Egypt who on 8 July launched an attack ending the truce and committing the Arab forces to another round of fighting.

In nine days leading up to a second truce the Israelis took the initiative, capturing the Arab towns of Nazareth, Lydda and Ramleh. Then, during the truce that followed Israel mobilised and trained more fighters, many of whom were newly arrived immigrants, and arranged the shipment of more weapons. It also consolidated its hold on the captured territories and, according to Bregman, razed 'Arab villages to the ground so that their previous inhabitants who took what they believed to be a temporary refuge elsewhere would have nowhere to return to' (2003: 57).

On 6 September, the Arab League led by Egypt decided to create an Arab government for Palestine based in Gaza with a small military force under its control. Shlaim (2005) suggests that this was undertaken for a number of reasons: to placate Arab popular opinion critical of Arab failures to protect the Palestinians, to provide a vehicle for challenging Abdullah's move to absorb the Arab part of Palestine, and to minimise the public outcry as the armies of the Arab League withdrew from the conflict. The government in Gaza was in essence a chimera with no political or military power and was not taken seriously by any of the parties to the conflict. Also during the second truce Count Bernadotte put forward another proposal for settling the conflict. Territorially it was similar to his previous proposal, although Jerusalem would fall under UN control, and the Palestinians would decide their own political fate in consultation with other Arab states. The proposal was due to be debated by the UN General Assembly on 21 September, but on 17 September Count Bernadotte was assassinated in Jerusalem, by members of the Israeli paramilitary group the Stern Gang under orders from a triumvirate that included Yitzak Shamir, who later became prime minister of Israel (Bregman, 2003).

During the second truce Ben-Gurion proposed to the Israeli cabinet the launching a major offensive to capture much of the West Bank, but failed to gain majority approval and switched his attention to a plan to push Egyptian forces back across the Negev into Egypt. At this time Shlaim (1999) claims that Israel received a peace proposal from the Egyptian government offering de facto recognition of Israel in exchange for Egypt's annexation of a portion of land in the Negev. He argues that Ben-Gurion ignored Egypt's proposals, and persuaded the cabinet to authorise a series of military offensives designed to capture the Negev. Over the next four months Israel picked off the Arab armies one by one, making large territorial gains. This began on 15 October when Israel broke the truce and launched Operation Yoav. In a week it captured Beersheba and Bayt Jibrin, with neither Transjordan nor the Arab legion intervening to support Egypt. On 29 October Israel launched a major offensive in the north code named Operation Hiram, which captured central Galilee. During the operation Shlaim (2005) claims that the IDF expelled large number of Arabs from the Galilee in line with recommendations made on 26 September by Ben-Gurion that should fighting resume in the north the Galilee should become 'clean' and 'empty' of Arabs.

A third UN truce came into effect on 31 October, which lasted until 22 December, when Israel again broke the truce by launching Operation Horev. This was highly successful, with the Israeli army driving the Egyptians out of the Negev and following it into Egypt proper. Eventually Britain intervened on the Egyptian side under the terms of the 1936 Anglo-Egyptian

Treaty, and after forceful pressure from President Truman Ben-Gurion agreed to withdraw his troops from the Sinai and accept a new truce.

POST-WAR NEGOTIATIONS: PEACE TREATIES, BORDERS AND REFUGEES

The war ended on 7 January 1949. It had extracted a high price on all parties. Israel had lost more than 6,000 lives or 1 per cent of its population. It had, however, made huge territorial gains. UN Resolution 181 had recommended the Jewish state be established in 57 per cent of mandatory Palestine. By the end of 1948 the Israeli state had control of 78 per cent.

After the war the Israelis engaged in immediate nation-building. Elections were held in January 1949 based on a system of proportional party lists. The Mapai party won the most seats with its leader Ben-Gurion becoming the nation's first prime minister, while Chaim Weizmann was installed as president. The Palestinians view the events of 1948 as so traumatic they are simply known as Al Nakba or 'The Catastrophe'. The refugees created prior to the start of the 'official war' on 15 May swelled during the conflict. The Israeli historian Illan Pappe, citing evidence from Benny Morris, writes that towards the end of the war 'several massacres were committed' by Israeli forces in the villages of 'Ilabun, Sa'sa'a, Dawamiyya, Sfsa and Zurief' and that these added 'an incentive to the flight of the population'. Pappe also notes that in the final stages of the conflict 'expulsion was even more systematic' (1999: 51–2).

The war ended with 520,000 Palestinian refugees, according to Israel, 726,000 as estimated by the UN, and 810,000 as estimated by the British government (Gilbert, 1999). The 150,000 Palestinians who were left in the new Israeli state were, according to Bregman, regarded by Israel as a 'dangerous and not-to-be-trusted potential fifth column' and were therefore placed under military rule:

> The military government operated in areas where Arabs were concentrated and its main task was to exercise governmental policies in these areas. It was a most powerful body hated by the Arabs, for it effectively controlled

> all spheres of their lives imposing on them severe restrictions: it banned the Arabs from leaving their villages and travel to other parts of the country without obtaining special permission; it detained suspects without trial and it also, frequently, in the name of security, closed whole areas, thus preventing Arab peasants access to their fields and plantations which was devastating for them for they were dependent on their crops for their livelihood. The military government also imposed curfews on whole villages and on one occasion, when the village of Kfar Qassem, unaware of the curfew, returned to their homes, the Israelis opened fire killing 47. (2003: 74)

During 1949 Israel, under the auspices of the UN, negotiated separate armistice agreements with all Arab states involved in the conflict. Jordan moved to annex the West Bank while Egypt moved to occupy the Gaza Strip but, unlike Jordan, it made no effort to annex the territory. The name Palestine had disappeared from the map, its territory having been absorbed into the Israeli and Jordanian states. In late April 1949 Israel met delegations from Egypt, Jordan, Syria, Lebanon and the Arab Higher Committee in Lausanne to try to hammer out a peace deal. The two central sticking points were borders and refugees. The Arab delegation wanted to see borders based on the 1947 UN partition resolution that they had previously rejected. The Israelis argued the permanent borders should be based on the ceasefire lines with only minor modifications. No agreement was reached.

On 11 December 1948, the UN General Assembly had passed Resolution 194, which resolved 'that the refugees wishing to return to their homes and live at peace with their neighbours should be permitted to do so at the earliest practicable date, and that compensation should be paid for the property of those choosing not to return and for loss of or damage to property'. This position on the repatriation of refugees, Pappe (1999) notes, was shared by the UN, Europe and the US. Israel rejected the return of refugees and the payment of compensation, arguing that the Arab states had created the refugee problem by attacking Israel and they should therefore settle the refugees in their own countries:

We did not want the war. Tel Aviv did not attack Jaffa. It was Jaffa which attacked Tel Aviv and this will not occur again. Jaffa will be a Jewish town. The repatriation of the Arabs is not justice, but folly. Those who declared war against us will have to bear the result after they have been defeated. (David Ben-Gurion, cited in Gabbay, 1959: 109)

Pappe argues that from June 1949 onwards Israeli leaders were committed to 'creating a fait accompli that would render repatriation impossible' (1999: 52). In that month Joseph Weitz wrote in a memorandum that there was a consensus among Israeli leaders that the best way to deal with the abandoned Palestinian villages was by 'destruction, renovation and settlement by Jews' (Weitz, cited in Pappe, 1999: 52). This plan, which Pappe claims Israel carried out 'to the letter', required the state 'to demolish what was left of abandoned Palestinian villages, almost 350 in all, so that the term repatriation itself, would become meaningless' (1999: 52). Pappe suggests that for Israelis the subject of the Palestinian refugees raises difficult questions about the nature of the Israeli state:

Israelis – leaders and people alike – have a genuine psychological problem when faced with the refugee issue. This is indeed for them the 'original sin'. It puts a huge question mark over the Israeli self-image of moral superiority and human sensitivity. It ridicules Israel's oxymorons, such as the 'purity of arms' or misnomers, such as the 'Israeli Defence Forces', and raises doubts over the religious notion of the 'chosen people' and the political pretension of being the only democracy in the Middle East which should be wholeheartedly supported by the West. In the past it has produced a series of repressions and self denials as well as the promotion of unrealistic political solutions ... It was accompanied by an intellectual struggle against the Palestinians, epitomised by the official Israeli fabrication of the history of the land and the conflict. (1999: 58)

Although the armistice agreements had ended the military conflict, there were no formal peace treaties signed between Israel and its Arab neighbours, setting the scene for further sporadic clashes. This failure to negotiate comprehensive peace treaties is a contentious issue. Sachar, for instance, blames Arab intransigence, claiming that Israel repeatedly attempted to make peace but its efforts were rebuffed by Arab states: '[The] Arab purpose was single minded and all-absorptive. It was flatly committed to the destruction of Israel as an independent state' (1977: 430). Some historians suggest the opposite. Shlaim notes that 'the files of the Israeli Foreign Ministry ... burst at the seams with evidence of Arab peace feelers and Arab readiness to negotiate with Israel from September 1948 on' (2000: 49).

In the years after 1948 the Arab world instituted an economic boycott against Israel, shut its borders and refused its aircraft permission to use their airspace. This period also saw a radical demographic shift in the Jewish population throughout the Middle East. In the nine years following the 1948 war 567,000 Jews left Muslim countries and most settled in Israel, so that the population swelled from 1,174,000 in 1949 to 1,873,000 in 1956 (Ovendale, 1999). Sachar (1977) claims that in many of these societies, particularly Iraq and Egypt, the Jewish population had 'prospered mightily', but argues that in the 1940s they were subject to increasing levels of harassment and persecution. He writes that in Libya anti-Jewish riots in 1945 had left several hundred dead or wounded, and in Syria the Jewish population saw its property and employment rights curtailed. Gilbert (1999) maintains that Israeli officials were instrumental in facilitating these population transfers from Muslim countries, known in Israel as 'the ingathering of the exiles', because there was a shortage of manpower in Israel after 1948. It has been claimed that the methods employed were controversial. Gilbert (1999) and Hirst (1977) write that in Iraq, Israeli agents planted bombs in synagogues and Jewish businesses in an attempt to stimulate immigration to Israel.

Despite the stabilisation of the political and military situation following the 1948 War clashes along the armistice lines were a constant source of friction between Israel and its Arab neighbours. Displaced Palestinians in Arab states began to engage in what was known as 'infiltration'. Shlaim comments that '90 per cent or more of all infiltrations were motivated by social and economic concerns' involving persons crossing the ceasefire lines to retrieve property, see relatives or tend their land (2000: 82). Many of the refugees had been separated from their homes and land and so had no employment and went hungry. The other 10 per cent involved acts of sabotage and violence directed against Israelis. Shlaim writes that the Israelis adopted a 'free fire' policy towards infiltrators, which encouraged the Arabs to organise into groups and respond in kind. The British Major John Glubb argued that 'the original infiltrators were harmless and unarmed seeking lost property or relatives. Yet Jewish terrorism [i.e. shoot to kill and reprisal raids] made the infiltrator into a gunman' (cited in Morris, 1997: 51).

Between the end of the 1948 War and the 1956 Suez War, the Israeli authorities estimated that 294 civilians had been killed by infiltrators from Jordan, Lebanon and Egypt (Morris, 1997: 97–8). Shlaim writes that in this period between 2,700 and 5,000 infiltrators, 'the great majority of them unarmed', were killed by 'trigger happy' Israeli soldiers (2000: 82). Some Israeli historians argue that Arab leaders encouraged infiltration as an attempt to weaken and destroy the Israeli state. In contrast Shlaim claims that 'there is strong evidence from Arab, British, American, UN and even Israeli sources to suggest that for the first six years after the war, the Arab governments were opposed to infiltration and tried to curb it' (2000: 84). Israel adopted a policy of reprisals directed against villages in Gaza and Jordan. Shlaim notes that 'all of these raids were aimed at civilian targets' and 'greatly inflamed Arab hatred of Israel and met with mounting criticism from the international community' (2000: 83).

A specialist reprisal brigade, unit 101, was created, under the command of Ariel Sharon. Its first major operation involved an attack on the village of Quibya in 1953, following the killing of an Israeli mother and two children by a hand grenade in Yahuda. Unit 101 reduced Quibya 'to a pile of rubble: forty-five houses had been blown up and sixty-nine civilians, two-thirds of them women and children' were killed (2000: 91). A UN report found that 'the inhabitants had been forced by heavy fire to stay inside, until their homes were blown up over them'

(2000: 91). Shlaim also writes that such acts were carried out against Arab villages within the State of Israel:

> Periodic search operations were also mounted in Arab villages inside Israel to weed out infiltrators. From time to time the soldiers who carried out these operations committed atrocities, among them gang rape, murder and on one occasion, the dumping of 120 infiltrators in the Arava desert without water. The atrocities were committed not in the heat of battle but for the most part against innocent civilians, including women and children. Coping with day to day security had a brutalising effect on the IDF. Soldiers in an army which prided itself on the precept of 'the purity of arms' showed growing disregard for human lives and carried out some barbaric acts that can only be described as war crimes. (2000: 83)

It was against this backdrop of border tensions that Israel became involved in a broader struggle between Britain, France and Egypt over control of the Suez Canal.

1956: THE SUEZ CONFLICT

In Egypt in 1952, Gamal Abd al-Nasser and his 'free officers' took power, following a bloodless coup, and turned the state into a republic. In 1954 Nasser became president and attempted to make himself the champion of a pan-Arabic renaissance and the leader of the decolonisation movement across the Middle East and Africa. Ovendale (1999) notes that the European colonial powers feared the effects of Nasser's Arab nationalism on their oil interests and geostrategic control of the Middle East and Africa. France was also hostile because of Nasser's support for Algerians fighting for independence. In July 1956 Nasser nationalised the Suez Canal after the US and Britain refused to fund the Aswan Dam Project, which Nasser saw as a means to develop Egypt as a modern nation. Britain and France, who were shareholders in the Canal, decided he had to be removed from power. Israel also wanted to see Nasser deposed, and between 22 and 24 October 1956 British, French and Israeli representatives met at Sèvres on the outskirts of Paris to devise a military plan to achieve that end (Shlaim,

2000). At this meeting the Israeli delegation also secured final approval for the supply of a nuclear reactor from France, which was delivered the following year and soon used to develop nuclear weapons.[15]

On 29 October 1956, the IDF launched an attack on Egyptian forces in the Sinai peninsula. The next day Britain and France issued an ultimatum to Egypt and Israel to withdraw their forces to a distance of ten miles from the Suez Canal. Israel complied, Egypt refused and the following day Britain and France began an aerial bombardment of the Egyptian airfields. Israel quickly secured an overwhelming military victory, capturing Gaza on 2 November and the whole Sinai peninsula three days later. On 7 November, Ben-Gurion delivered a speech to the Knesset where 'he hinted that Israel planned to annex the entire Sinai peninsula as well as the Straits of Tiran' (Shlaim, 2000: 179). However, under strong pressure from the USA and USSR and threats of UN sanctions, Israel was eventually forced to withdraw from all of the Sinai after six months.

Israel's motivations have been the subject of much controversy. One version maintains that Israel was driven to attack Egypt for three main reasons. First, it is argued the Egyptian leader Nasser was planning to lead a combined Arab force (Egypt, Jordan, Syria) in an attempt to destroy Israel, and the Suez conflict was necessary as a pre-emptive military strike to prevent this. Sachar (1977) points to belligerent speeches made by Arab leaders in the months preceding the war, which he argues were proof of imminent Arab plans to destroy Israel. He also suggests that Egypt's acquisition of a large shipment of arms from Czechoslovakia in 1955 had shifted the balance of power against Israel. Sachar also claims that Israel wanted to break Egypt's blockade of the Suez Canal, and stop Palestinian guerrilla attacks on Israel. This perspective on Israeli motivations sees the attack on Egypt as defensive in orientation and concerned only with strengthening the country's security situation.

Other historians have pointed to different reasons for the attack. Shlaim (2000) argues that Israel's military establishment, led by Ben-Gurion and Moshe Dayan, was determined to goad

..ber of troops into the Sinai, bordering Israel and asked the ..N troops who formed a buffer between the two countries to evacuate their positions. The Egyptian troops then moved into Sharm al-Shaykh and proclaimed a blockade of the Israeli port of Eliat, which was accessible only through Egyptian waters.

Two weeks later, at 7.45 a.m. on 5 June 1967, Israel launched an aerial attack on Egyptian airfields, destroying 298 warplanes, the bulk of the Egyptian air force, in a single day. Israeli ground forces also launched an almost simultaneous land invasion of Egyptian territory, forcing their way to the Suez Canal and capturing the Sinai peninsula in two days. At noon on 5 June, as part of a defence pact with Egypt, Syrian, Jordanian and Iraqi forces attacked targets inside Israel. Within two hours the air forces of all three were destroyed by the Israeli air force, as well as an Iraqi military base near the Jordanian border. Jordanian land forces also intervened in support of Egypt. Jordanian artillery shelled Israeli towns and moved troops into Arab East Jerusalem. Israel then drove the Jordanian army out of the West Bank and East Jerusalem, occupying them both by 7 June. The following day Israeli warplanes attacked the American spy ship, the USS *Liberty*, with cannon, missiles and napalm, killing 34 US service personnel and injuring 171.[16] On 9 June, Israel attacked Syria, despite strong UN pressure, and occupied the Golan Heights. There have been allegations in the Israeli press that about a thousand unresisting Egyptian soldiers, as well as dozens of unarmed Palestinian refugees, were killed by the Israeli army during the war (*Ha'aretz,* 17 August 1995, cited in *Washington Report on Middle East Affairs*, February/March 1996).

The war was an overwhelming military success for Israel. In six days it had destroyed three Arab armies and made large territorial gains, capturing the Sinai peninsula, the Golan Heights, the West Bank, Gaza Strip and Arab East Jerusalem. The reasons behind Israel's decision to launch the offensive are disputed. The official Israeli cabinet documents stated that the 'Government [of Israel] ascertained that the armies of Egypt, Syria and Jordan are deployed for immediate multi-front aggression, threatening the very existence of the state' (cited

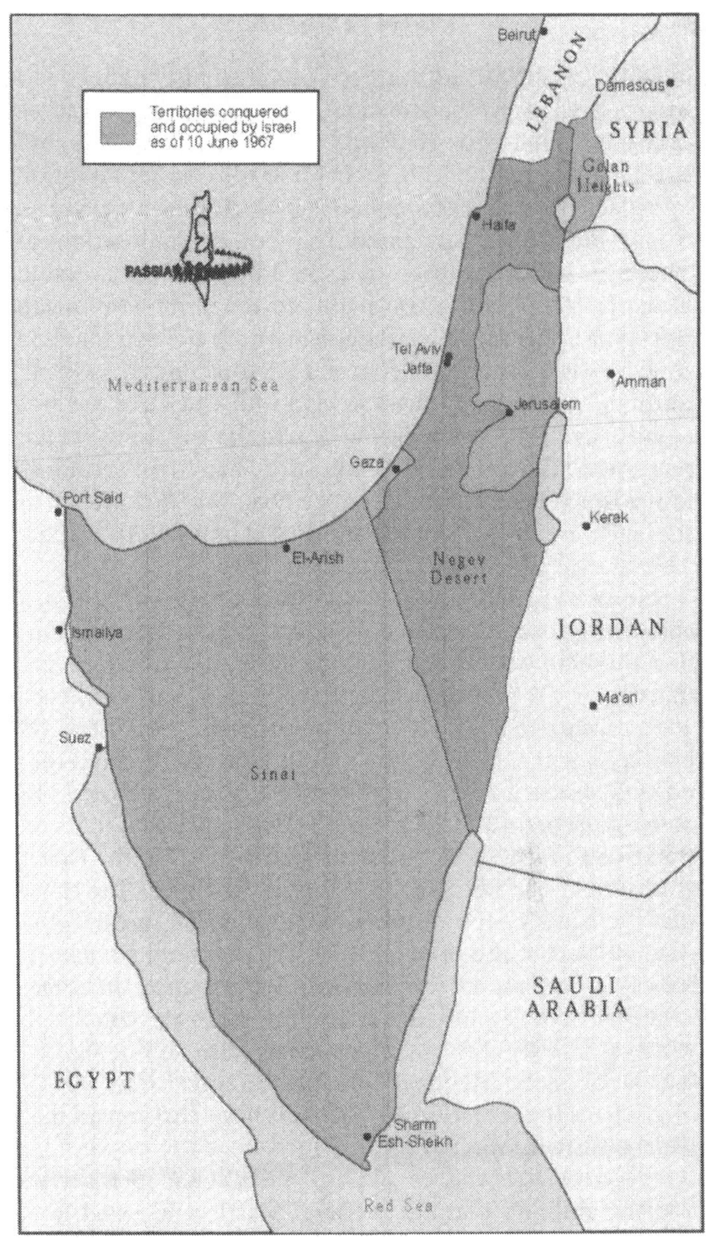

Map 3 The Near East After the 1967 June War

in Finkelstein, 2001: 130). Three years previously Arab leaders had declared in an official document their intention to achieve 'collective military preparations' for the 'final liquidation of Israel' (Shlaim, 2000: 230). Sachar points to Nasser's decision to replace UN peacekeeping troops in the Sinai with Egyptian troops, and military preparations by other Arab nations as evidence that 'the garrot ... was rapidly tightening around Israel' (1977: 632). He also points to Israeli motivations to stop Syrian shelling of Israeli settlements in the demilitarised zone between Israel and Syria, and guerrilla raids into Israeli territory. Another justification given for Israel's attack was Egypt's decision to blockade the Straits of Tiran, which prevented access to the Israeli port of Eliat. This, according to the Israeli Foreign Minister Abba Eban, was an 'attempt at strangulation', which constituted an 'act of war' (Eban, 1992: 334, cited in Finkelstein, 2001: 137).

Some other historians have questioned these explanations and pointed to an alternative set of motivations. The assertions that the Arab states were planning an imminent attack and that they had the military strength to threaten Israel's existence are both disputed. Finkelstein notes that an 'exhaustive US intelligence at the end of the month [May 1967] could find no evidence that Egypt was planning to attack' (2001: 134). Menachem Begin and Yitzak Rabin later argued that the Arab states had not been planning an attack and that the Israeli government had been aware of this at the time.[17] The claim that the combined Arab armies posed a mortal threat to the state of Israel is also disputed. The CIA produced a report in May 1967 forecasting, with remarkable prescience, that Israel would win a war against one or all of the Arab states combined, whoever attacked first, in about a week. British intelligence had reached the identical conclusion (Finkelstein, 2001). Menachem Begin and Ezer Weizmann have also argued that Israel's existence was never threatened.[18]

Five years after the war, in an Israeli newspaper article, a senior military planner, General Mattityahu Peled, was dismissive of the Arab threat in 1967:

There is no reason to hide the fact that since 1949 no one dared, or more precisely, no one was able to threaten the very existence of Israel. In spite of that, we have continued to foster a sense of our own inferiority, as if we were a weak and insignificant people, which, in the midst of an anguished struggle for its existence, could be exterminated at any moment ... it is notorious that the Arab leaders themselves, thoroughly aware of their own impotence, did not believe in their own threats ... I am sure that our General Staff never told the government that the Egyptian military threat represented any threat to Israel or that we were unable to crush Nasser's army, which with unheard of foolishness, had exposed itself to the devastating might of our army ... To claim that the Egyptian forces concentrated on our borders were capable of threatening Israel's existence not only insults the intelligence of anyone capable of analysing this kind of situation, but is an insult to the Zahal [the Israeli army]. (*Ma'ariv*, 24 March 1972, cited in Hirst, 1977: 211)

Other posited explanations for Israel's decision to attack its Arab neighbours include a desire to safeguard the deterrent image of the IDF. Shlaim (2000) suggests that the Egyptian blockade represented a threat to Israel's 'iron wall' of militarised strength. Others suggest different motivations. Neff writes that on the eve of the 1967 War the CIA had identified three Israeli objectives: 'the destruction of the centre of power of the radical Arab socialist movements' [i.e. Nasser's regime], 'the destruction of the arms of the radical Arabs', and the 'destruction of both Jordan and Syria as modern States' (Neff, 1985: 230, cited in Finkelstein, 2001: 143). Hirst (1977) argues that Israeli military planners had been preparing the attack since they were forced to leave the Sinai in 1956, and cites comments from General Burns, the chief of staff of the United Nations Truce Supervision Organization (UNTSO) in the early 1960s, that Israel would probably seek to go to war again soon to break the Arab economic blockade and overcome its own economic difficulties.

Another explanation that has been cited as a motivation for Israel's decision involved a desire to expand the boundaries of the state. Proponents of this view point to comments made by the Israeli commander Yigal Allon on the eve of the 1967 war that 'in the case of a new war' Israel must seek as a central aim 'the territorial fulfilment of the land of Israel' (cited in Finkelstein, 2001: 143). There is evidence since the 1950s in the writings of David Ben-Gurion and other Israeli leaders that there had been a desire to expand Israel to incorporate all of Jerusalem and the West Bank. The Israeli historian Benny Morris notes:

> A strong expansionist current ran through both Zionist ideology and Israeli society. There was a general feeling shared by prominent figures as Dayan and Ben-Gurion, that the territorial gains of the 1948 war had fallen short of the envisioned promised land. Bechiya Le Dorot – literally a cause for lamentation for future generations – was how Ben-Gurion described the failure to conquer Arab East Jerusalem; leading groups in Israeli society regarded the Jordanian controlled West Bank with the same feeling. (Morris, 1989: 410–11, cited in Finkelstein, 2001: 221)

The conflict triggered a second mass exodus of Palestinians, many of whom became refugees for a second time, as they had sought refuge in the West Bank and Gaza after having to abandon their homes in 1948–49. Nur Masalha, senior lecturer at the Holy Land Research Project at the University of Surrey, argues that 'there is no evidence to suggest that there were wholesale or blanket expulsion orders adopted or carried out by the Israeli army in June 1967, although the policy of selective eviction, demolition and encouragement of "transfer" continued for several weeks after the Israeli army occupied the West Bank and Gaza Strip' (Masalha, 1999: 100). Masalha maintains that in 1967 'evictions and demolitions were evident in numerous geographical locations in the West Bank' and that 'young men from several cities and refugee camps were also targeted for deportation' (1999: 101). Peter Dodd and Halim Barakat in their study of the 1967 exodus, *River without Bridges*, provide similar explanations for the exodus:

> The exodus was a response to the severe situational pressures existing at the time. The situational pressures were generated by the aerial attacks upon a defenceless country, including the extensive use of napalm, the occupation of the West Bank villages by the Israeli army, and the actions of the occupying

forces. Certainly the most dramatic of these was the eviction of civilians, and the deliberate destruction of a number of villages [Imwas, Yalu, Bayt Nuba, Bayt Marsam, Bayt Awa, Habla, al-Burj and Jiftlik]. Other action, such as threats and the mass detention of male civilians, also created situational pressures. (Dodd & Barakat, 1969: 54, cited in Masalha, 1999: 96)

William Wilson Harris (1980), who reached similar conclusions in his analysis of the exodus, estimates that 250,000 residents of the West Bank, 70,000 residents of the Gaza Strip and 90,000 residents of the Golan Heights were forced to flee their homes during 1967. The displaced residents of the West Bank were prevented from returning to the area by harsh measures. Testimony in the Israeli press, from an unnamed soldier serving in the 5th Reserve Division on the Jordan River, details the fate of displaced Palestinians attempting to return to their homes:

We fired such shots every night on men, women and children. Even during moonlit nights when we could identify the people, that is distinguish between men, women and children. In the mornings we searched the area and, by explicit order from the officer on the spot, shot the living, including those who hid or were wounded, again including the women and children. (*Haolam Haze*, 10 October 1967, cited in Masalha, 1999: 99)

There were reports that after the war Israel began destroying Palestinian homes in the newly occupied territories. The American historian Alfred Lilienthal claims that

according to UN figures, the Israelis destroyed during the period between 11 June 1967 and 15 November 1969 some 7,554 Palestinian Arab homes in the territories seized during that war; this figure excluded 35 villages in the occupied Golan Heights that were razed to the ground. In the two years between September 1969 and 1971 the figure was estimated to have reached 16,312 homes. (1978: 160)

On 19 June 1967, Israeli leaders formulated an offer to hand back the Golan Heights, the Sinai and the Gaza Strip in return for demilitarisation agreements, peace treaties and assurance of navigation rights from Egypt, Syria and Jordan. Bregman (2003) suggests that the decision, taken two months later, by Arab leaders meeting in Khartoum to issue the famous 'three nos' to peace, recognition and negotiations with Israel led to the Israeli decision taken on 30 October to officially withdraw the offer, and harden its attitude. Shlaim (2000) disagrees, arguing that there was no evidence that the conditional offer of withdrawal was ever presented to the Arab states, and that the offer was almost immediately killed by political and military leaders in Israel who wanted to retain a large part of the captured territories, and who began in mid-July to approve plans for constructing settlements on the occupied Golan Heights. He maintains that the 'three nos' at Khartoum referred to 'no formal peace *treaty*, but not a rejection of a state of peace; no *direct* negotiations, but not a refusal to talk through third parties; and no *de jure* recognition of Israel, but acceptance of its existence as a state' (2000: 258). Shlaim suggests the conference was 'a victory for Arab moderates who argued for trying to obtain the withdrawal of Israeli forces by political rather than military means' (2000: 258). There have also been claims that Israel turned down a peace treaty with Egypt and Jordan at the conference.[19]

Shlaim notes that there was no Israeli debate about handing back East Jerusalem, but that Israeli leaders were split on how much of the West Bank they wanted to retain. He suggests outright annexation was favoured by only a few, because it would mean absorbing large numbers of Arabs into the Jewish state. Most of these leaders preferred one of two options. The 'Allon Plan', put forward by the Israel Deputy Prime Minister Yigal Allon, proposed limited autonomy for Palestinians in part of the West Bank (Israel would still own the land and control security in the autonomy area), with Israel taking control of a large strip of the Jordan Valley, much of the area around Jerusalem and the Judean desert. These parts of the West Bank would then be colonised with Jewish settlements and army bases. The second option involved handing back to Jordan part of the West Bank, with Israel keeping approximately a third

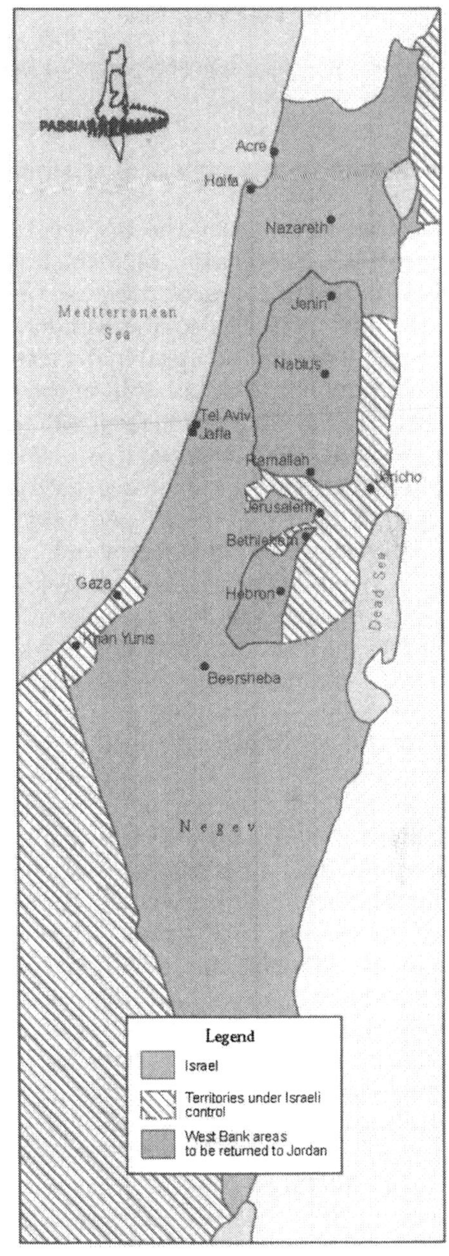

Map 4 The Allon Plan, July 1967

of the area. Neither proposal was acceptable to King Hussein or the Palestinians.

RESOLUTION 242 AND THE WAR OF ATTRITION

The 1967 War was followed by the UN Security Council unanimously adopting Resolution 242, which has become the framework document for successive attempts to resolve the conflict. The resolution called for the 'withdrawal of Israeli armed forces from territories occupied in the recent conflict' in line with the principle 'emphasise[d]' in the preambular paragraph of the 'inadmissibility of the acquisition of territory by war'. It also 'emphasised' the 'need to work for a just and lasting peace in which every State in the area can live in security' as well as a 'just settlement of the refugee problem' and the establishment of navigation rights. Egypt and Jordan agreed to Resolution 242 while Syria rejected it. The Palestinians also rejected it on the grounds that it only spoke of their plight as a refugee problem, making no mention of their rights to self-determination and national sovereignty. Israel accepted the resolution in 1970.

The meaning of the withdrawal clause has been contested. Israel has argued that because the definite article 'the' was not included in the English version of the resolution ('from territories occupied' rather than 'from the territories occupied') it means that the scope of withdrawal was left vague and that Israel did not have to withdraw from all the territories it occupied in the conflict. Israel has also argued that many of the nations that endorsed the resolution, including the US, UK, USSR and Brazil, agreed that Israel did not have to withdraw from all the territories (Israeli Ministry of Foreign Affairs, 1999). Finkelstein (2001) disputes this. He points to statements made by the United Nations General Assembly president that 'there is virtual unanimity in upholding the principle that conquest of territory by war is inadmissible in our time under the Charter' (UN General Assembly 1967, cited in Finkelstein, 2001: 145). This affirmation, the president continued, was 'made in virtually all statements' and noted that 'virtually all speakers laid down the corollary that withdrawal of forces to their original position is expected' (UN General Assembly 1967a, cited in Finkelstein, 2001: 145). The debates at the UN Security Council, Finkelstein argues, were similarly unambiguous, with almost all representatives stressing both the inadmissibility clause and the need for a complete Israeli withdrawal.[20] He also argues that the American position was for a full Israeli withdrawal.[21]

Having failed to secure such a withdrawal from the occupied territories, Egypt fought the 'war of attrition' against Israel between 1967 and 1970. Shlaim argues that President Nasser's immediate purpose was to 'prevent the conversion of the Suez Canal into a de facto border, while his ultimate goal was to force Israel to withdraw to the pre-war border' (2000: 289). Egypt bombed Israeli troop concentrations in the occupied Sinai and Palestinian guerrillas launched cross-border attacks against Israel. Israel then attacked military and civilian targets within Egypt and Jordan. Numerous Egyptian coastal towns and cities were heavily damaged by Israeli air attacks. The Israeli commander Ezer Weizman recalled the fate of Egyptian border city Ismailia, which the Israeli army bombarded 'incessantly, devastating it from the air as well as with land-based artillery', so that aerial photographs 'showed its western portions resembling the cities at the end of World War II' (Weizman, cited in Gilbert, 1999: 410). Moshe Dayan was later to claim that Israeli attacks during the war of attrition had created one and a half million Egyptian refugees as well as emptying the entire Jordan Valley of its inhabitants (*Al Hamishar*, 10 May 1978). The war was finally brought to a halt in August 1970 when both sides agreed to a US-sponsored ceasefire. Morris (1992) estimates that in the three years of conflict, 367 Israeli soldiers and more than 10,000 Egyptian soldiers and civilians were killed.

SETTLEMENT-BUILDING, ECONOMIC INTEGRATION AND THE OCCUPATION

In the aftermath of the 1967 War Israel established settlements on the newly captured territories and placed the Palestinian residents under military rule. Two major reasons were given for the creation of settlements. One stressed their security value:

> There was also a strategic justification for not wanting to give up the occupied West Bank and that was that it turned Israel's 'narrow waist' into something wider. Before seizing the West Bank Israel's width at some parts measured scarcely nine miles from the Jordan bulge to the Mediterranean, and by clinging to the occupied territories west of the Jordan river Israel made it more difficult for a potential Arab invasion force coming from the east to cut in two. (Bregman, 2003: 126–7)

Some Israelis were dismissive of the security argument, alleging it was a pretext to satisfy international public opinion. One official, writing in the Israeli press, claimed that 'we have to use the pretext of security needs and the authority of the military governor as there is no way of driving out the Arabs from their land so long as they refuse to go and accept our compensation' (*Ha'aretz*, 23 November 1969, cited in Hirst, 1977: 241).

A second strand of thought justified settlement-building and retention of the occupied territories, on the basis of divine rights. Victory in the Six-Day War was seen by many religious Jews as a sign of support from God and evidence that the messianic era was at hand, leading to a surge in support for religious nationalism. A number of new parties and organisations were formed that advocated permanent control and settlement of the West Bank and Gaza Strip because, it was argued, these areas were a central component of the biblical land of Israel.

Harold Fisch, the former rector of Israel's Bar-Ilan University, argues that God promised Abraham the land of Israel as an eternal possession, and this provides justification for sovereignty over the West Bank and Gaza Strip:

> The covenant between the people of Israel and its God, which includes the promised land as an integral part, is an important objective within the entire scheme of creation. It is from this fact that the linkage between the people of Israel and its land is rooted – in the transcendental will of God who created all in his honor. (Fisch, 1982: 189)

These arguments are echoed in more contemporary comments. In an interview in the *Observer*, Ariel Sharon, the Israeli prime minister, was quoted as saying 'Israel is the promised land – promised to Jews and no-one else' (13 July 2003). The viewpoint has also gained ground in the US via the Christian fundamentalist movement, who are key supporters of George W. Bush and the Republicans. In a 2002 programme the BBC interviewed the pastor of a major church in Texas who explained his view that:

> Well, you understand that the Jewish state was something that's born in the mind of God and we are a people who believe the scripture and the scripture says very clearly that God created Israel, that God is the protector and defender of Israel. If God created Israel, if God defends Israel, is it not logical to say that those who fight with Israel are fighting with God? (BBC Radio 4, *A Lobby to be Reckoned With*, 7 May 2002)

Other arguments for Israel's rights to keep and settle the lands captured in 1967 included the position that since the land has changed sovereignty many times over the last 2,000 years, the Jews have as much claim as any others who had controlled it since they were exiled.[22] Some Israelis have also argued that because the Palestinians rejected partition in 1947 they have given up their rights to a share of mandatory Palestine. Others point to the legal status of the Balfour Declaration or argue that since Israel won the territories in a 'war of self-defence' they have a right to keep them. Binyamin Netanyahu argues that to prevent Jews from building settlements in the occupied territories is a form of apartheid:

> Careful manipulation of the media by the Arabs has left many Westerners with the indelible impression that Arab paupers are being kicked off their hovels in droves to make way for Jewish suburbs in the 'densely populated West Bank.'... For what is manifestly occurring is that the West, which so sharply condemned anti-black apartheid in South Africa, is being used by the Arabs as an enforcer of anti-Jewish apartheid that pertains in the Arab's own countries. (2000: 189–92)

In a review of Israel's settlement-building programmes Israel Shahak and Norton Mezvinsky (1999) note that until 1974 Moshe Dayan oversaw settlement activity. His policy was to limit settlements primarily to Hebron, northern Sinai and the Jordan Valley, as part of a bargain he made with the Palestinian feudal notables who controlled the villages. After 1974, Shahak and Mezvinsky note that religious settler groups, primarily Gush Emunim, and their political allies in the Knesset came to the fore in determining settlement policy, with the support of both Labor and particularly the Likud party. In 1973 Israel introduced the Galili Plan, which Shafir suggests transformed the Allon plan's '*military frontier* to a combination of a *messianic frontier* and a *suburban frontier*' (1999: 92). Some commentators have pointed to the extreme ideological views of many religious settlers, which justify attacks on Palestinians and attempts to expel them from their homes and land in what is seen as a process of 'purification' or 'sanctification' of the land.[23] Hirst has suggested that even prior to 1974, the creation of settlements was at the expense of Palestinians:

> Sometimes it was necessary to uproot an entire village – though not necessarily all at once. For years the impoverished inhabitants of Beit Askariyah watched in impotent dismay as the great cantonments of the Kfar Etzion settlement went up around them, relentlessly encroaching on their agricultural and grazing land before swallowing up their homes too. In January 1972, the army expelled 6,000 Bedouins from Rafah in north-east Sinai. It demolished their houses, poisoned their wells, and kept them at bay with a barbed wire fence. The Bedouins were eventually employed as night watchmen or labourers – on their own property and in the service of those who had taken it from them. (1977: 242)

In 1981 the Likud administration introduced the Drobless Plan. Shafir suggests that its purpose was to 'scatter Jewish settlements among Arab towns and villages in order to ensure that no homogenous Palestinian inhabited area, the potential core of a Palestinian state would remain' (1999: 92). In a more recent study Amnesty International (1999c) examined how settlement-building and Palestinian house demolitions are 'inextricably linked with Israeli policy to control and colonize areas of the West Bank', a policy that has been 'energetically followed for over 30 years by all administrations from 1967 until the present time'. The process of colonisation, the report continues, depends 'not just on finding land that is physically "suitable", but on alienating it from the Palestinians, defending it against Palestinian use, and ensuring through such processes as registration and leasing that Palestinians are disqualified from having any future benefit from that land'. Amnesty International argues that the damage to the 'tight knit pattern of Palestinian villages' has been 'pervasive'. Settlement-building is prohibited by the Fourth Geneva Convention, article 49 of which stipulates that 'the occupying power shall not deport or transfer parts of its own population into the territory it occupies'. The Israeli government has disputed this, arguing that the area is 'administered' rather than 'occupied' and that article 49 of the convention has 'no bearing' on the Israeli settlements because the convention was intended to cover forced transfers during the Second World War, whereas 'the movement of individuals to these areas is entirely voluntary, while the settlements themselves are not intended to displace Arab inhabitants, nor do they do so in practice' (Israeli Ministry of Foreign Affairs, 1996).

The practice has, however, been repeatedly condemned by the European Union and the United Nations, who in multiple resolutions have deemed the settlements illegal and in need of removal. The practice was condemned in December 2000 (UN Resolution 55/132) by 152 votes to 4 (Israel, United States, Micronesia, Marshall Islands).

In Jerusalem, Israel initiated a policy of 'Judaisation' in an attempt to change the demographic, physical, cultural, legal and economic status of the city. It appropriated Arab land in the city and demolished Arab housing. In the Jewish Quarter prior to 1948, approximately 20 per cent of the property was Jewish-owned. After 1967, Hirst writes, Israelis 'relentlessly forced out the 5,500 [Arab] inhabitants who lived there' (1977: 235). The demolitions and evictions occurred all over the city, with the victims of land expropriations receiving either inadequate levels of compensation or sometimes none. Moves to change the legal and demographic structure of Jerusalem have drawn criticism from the international community. In 1999 the UN condemned such actions by 139 votes to 1 (Israel).[24] Hirst also notes that Arab culture was suppressed or denigrated, especially in schools.[25]

The Israeli state quickly moved to integrate the Arabs living in the occupied territories into the Israeli economy. Some historians, for example Sachar, suggest that for Palestinians this was a generally beneficial process, creating 'unprecedented affluence' as part of a 'comparatively painless' occupation (1977: 688–9). Other Israelis were critical of this process, arguing that Israel was instituting colonial policies in which a powerful Israeli minority was exploiting a captive Arab population for the use of its cheap labour and its role as a market for Israeli products:

> Better men than I have enlarged on the grim paradox that threatens the Zionist vision, the social and moral failure of that vision, which are to be expected from the transformation of the Jews into employers, managers and supervisors of Arab hewers of wood and drawers of water, and all of it plus the slogan of 'Integration' ... There is an inescapable process in a population that is divided into two peoples, one dominant, the other dominated. No! The State of Israel will not be such a monstrosity. (Ya'akov Talmon, cited in Sachar, 1977: 713)

There has also been commentary in the Israeli press suggesting the conditions under which the Palestinians were obliged to work for Israelis were exploitative and humiliating. Palestinians with jobs in Israel were not legally allowed to spend the night there so that many had to be bussed in over long distances from the occupied territories. This sometimes extended their working day to 17 hours. The Israeli magazine *Haolam Haze* reported on those that were permitted to sleep illegally on Israeli farms: 'Too far away for the eye to see, hidden in the orchards, there are the sheep pens for the servants, of a sort that even a state like South Africa would be ashamed of' (22 December 1982, cited in Chomsky, 1999: 141). In a *Jerusalem Post* interview, the

Israeli journalist Aryeh Rubinstein asks Amos Hadar, secretary general of the Moshav [agricultural] movement, whether he agrees with the use of Arab labour, 'but only on condition that they will live in subhuman conditions, degraded, and not under human conditions, more or less?' 'Correct', replies Hadar stressing that 'there is a difficult question here'. 'There is no choice but to employ Arabs', but they must be bussed in and out of Israel every day. 'It is hard, it is costly, it is problematic from an economic standpoint but there is no other solution' (26 December 1982, cited in Chomsky, 1999: 141).

There has also been criticism of Israeli use of Arab child labour. Israel's Arabic-language communist newspaper *Al-Ittihad* described a child labour market at Jaffa:

> In this market foremen get rich by exploiting the labour of children and young men from the occupied areas. Every morning at 4 a.m. cars from Gaza and the Strip start arriving there, bringing dozens of Arab workers who line up in the street in a long queue. A little later at 4.30 a.m. Arab boys who work in restaurants in the town begin to arrive. These boys work in restaurants for a month on end, including Saturdays ... Dozens, indeed hundreds of boys, who should be at school come from Gaza to work in Israel. The cars can be seen coming and going from earliest dawn. At about 6 a.m. Israeli labour brokers start arriving to choose 'working donkeys' as they call them. They take great care over their choice, actually feeling the 'donkeys' muscles. (30 April 1973, cited in Hirst, 1977: 246)

MILITARY OCCUPATION/ADMINISTRATION

Israel imposed a military administration on the occupied territories, which seriously restricted the social and political rights of its residents. According to the United Nations and human rights groups, it also involved extensive human rights violations. Israel argued that the policies were necessary to protect the state from attacks by infiltrators or Palestinians in the occupied territory, who they claimed were susceptible to PLO incitement. Morris suggests that severe repression coupled with 'massive use' of informers and collaborators by the Israeli security service Shin Bet meant that armed activity by the PLO in the occupied territories was 'virtually eradicated' by 1971 (1992: 279). Some commentators, including Chomsky, have suggested that the imposition of such policies had another objective. This was to make life difficult for the Palestinians in the occupied territories, so that they would emigrate and allow Israel to absorb the parts of the occupied territories that it wanted, without having to worry about a large Arab population that would 'dilute' the Jewish character of the Israeli state. Chomsky points to the official government records of a meeting at the start of the Israeli occupation in September 1967, when Moshe Dayan urged government ministers to tell the Palestinian residents of the occupied territories that 'we have no solution, that you shall continue to live like dogs, and whoever wants to can leave – and we will see where this process leads ... In five years we may have 200,000 less people – and that is a matter of enormous importance' (Beilin, 1985, cited in Chomsky, 1992: 434). Professor Ian Lustick suggests that Israel also wanted to break up the territorial continuity of Israeli Arab villages in the Galilee and points to the 1976 Koenig memorandum in which the Israeli minister of the interior recommended the 'coordination of a smear campaign against Rakah activists ... the harassment of "all negative personalities at all levels and at all institutions" and the employment of techniques for encouraging the emigration of Arab intellectuals, and for downgrading the effectiveness of Arab university student organizations' (1980: 56). It is widely argued that the policies Israel instituted breached international law. They also led to it being frequently condemned at the UN General Assembly and Security Council by near unanimous votes.[26] These policies included the systematic torture of prisoners,[27] imprisonment without trial,[28] collective punishments,[29] the taking of natural resources, curfews and searches,[30] house demolitions and deportations. The practices have also attracted criticism from human rights groups:

Amnesty International has for many years documented and condemned violations of international human rights and humanitarian law by Israel directed against the Palestinian population of the Occupied Territories. They include unlawful killings; torture and ill-treatment; arbitrary detention; unfair trials; collective punishments such as punitive closures of areas and destruction of homes; extensive and wanton destruction of property; deportations; and discriminatory treatment as compared to Israeli settlers. Most of these violations are grave breaches of the Fourth Geneva Convention and are therefore war crimes. Many have also been committed in a widespread and systematic manner, and in pursuit of government policy; such violations meet the definition of crimes against humanity under international law. (Amnesty International, 2002a)

NATIONALISM AND THE RISE OF THE OPPOSITION MOVEMENTS

In the aftermath of 1948, the refugees who were displaced had begun to formulate a vision of 'the return'. Initially it was hoped that the United Nations or the Arab states themselves would help the refugees to achieve this objective. However, as the years passed the lack of concrete progress began to frustrate the refugees and they became increasingly disillusioned by the leaders of the Arab states. By 1964 Yasser Arafat had established a small guerrilla organisation, Fatah, which was granted a secure base by Syria's radical Ba'athist regime. Fatah's philosophy from the outset was to mobilise popular Arab support behind guerrilla operations of increasing scale and intensity conducted against Israel. Prior to the 1967 War, Hirst (1977) alleges that Egypt, Jordan and Lebanon had all tried to prevent guerrilla incursions into Israel, but that after the war this became more difficult as popular support for guerrilla operations increased. By February 1968 Fatah members had taken control of the National Council of the PLO and Arafat became chairman. The aftermath of the war also saw the formation of Dr George Habash's PFLP (Popular Front for the Liberation of Palestine), which began to build a strong base of support in the refugee camps of the Gaza Strip.

In March 1968, Israeli forces launched an attack on the Karameh refugee camp in Jordan. Israel claimed the attack w… ıd in retaliation for PLO attacks, which had killed six peopl… ked wounded 44. Fifteen thousand troops backed by tank… forces the camp. Rather than retreat to the hills the g…

stayed, fought and suffered huge losses. Half the Palestinian guerrillas, 150 in all, were killed, together with 128 members of the Jordanian army and 29 Israeli soldiers (Hirst, 1977). Although the guerrillas had lost many fighters it was considered a significant victory because the Israelis had suffered unusually high casualties and met fierce resistance. The battle of Karameh led to an influx of volunteers from across the Arab world to join the guerrilla movements. In the years after 1967, as well as engaging in a guerrilla war, the Palestinians began to formulate a view of what a future Palestinian entity would look like. The result of this was the vision of the 'Democratic State of Palestine' put forward by the PLO planner and negotiator Nabil Shaath in 1969. The new state, it was hoped, would involve the dismantling of the Israeli state and its replacement with a non-sectarian Palestine in which Christian, Muslim and Jew would live together in equality (Hirst, 1977). It would include the Jews already residing there and the Palestinians who had been displaced in 1948 and 1967.

These proposals were not immediately or universally accepted by Palestinians. Hirst (1977) suggests that some saw them as capitulation to the enemy or at best premature considering that Israel was still militarily dominant. Others feared that the more technologically advanced Israelis would dominate them, while some considered it a tactical propaganda move aimed at international opinion.[31] The concept was a complete non-starter for almost all the Jewish population of Israel. The country had been constructed out of Palestine with huge military and diplomatic effort, and there was no desire to dilute its Jewish character. Furthermore Israelis were fearful of the extreme anti-Jewish rhetoric emanating from its Arab neighbours and worried that any returning refugees might want to take revenge for being displaced from their lands. The former head of Israeli military intelligence, Yehoshavat Harkabi, argued that the concept was a propaganda device designed to mask a struggle that was still 'genocidal' in intent. T[illegible] idea was eventually dropped after 1974 when the PLO mo[illegible] towards a two-state solution.

In the two years after the 1967 War the forces of Fatah and the other guerrilla movements had grown from 300 to more than 30,000, and substantial funding was coming in from the Arab world. The number of operations also increased dramatically. Fatah records claim that 98 per cent of these occurred outside the State of Israel with two-thirds of them occurring in the West Bank. Fatah regularly insisted that the army and 'Zionist institutions' were its real targets, not civilians (especially women and children), and if these were attacked it was in response to attacks on Palestinian civilians, and was selectively done. However, Hirst (1977) points out that although the 'great bulk' of attacks were aimed at military targets, civilians were unquestionably targeted. Bombs were planted in supermarkets in Jerusalem and bus stops in Tel-Aviv and rockets were fired on settlements in Kiryat Shmoneh and Eilat. While Fatah confined its actions to historic Palestine, the PFLP did not. It attacked targets all over the world. It hijacked foreign airliners. It firebombed branches of Marks & Spencer because of their fundraising for Israel. It blew up an Arab oil pipeline because the extraction was by an American oil company on behalf of a 'feudal' Arab monarchy. The main purpose of these actions, George Habash maintained, was publicity:

> When we hijack a plane it had more effect than if we killed a hundred Israelis in battle. For decades world public opinion has been neither for nor against the Palestinians. It simply ignored us. At least the world is talking about us now. (*Der Stern*, 19 September 1970, cited in Hirst, 1977: 304)

However, the opposition movements were to suffer a major blow in 1970. The PLO had established its headquarters in Jordan, where many Palestinian refugees who had been displaced in the wars of 1948 and 1967 had fled. There, the organisation had formed a state-within-a-state, which openly threatened the rule of the Hashemite monarchy. Following an assassination attempt on King Hussein and a series of hijackings carried out by the PFLP, the king set his army on the guerrillas. In ten days of bloody struggle, thousands of guerrillas were killed, and within a year most of th political elements of the Palestinian movement were expelled and ended up in Lebanon. 'Black September', as it became known among Palestinians, produced an organisation bearing the same name. Its most well-known operation was the taking of Israeli athletes as hostages at the 1972 Munich Olympics. Eight members of Black September took eleven Israelis hostage at the Olympic village in Munich, demanding the release of 200 Palestinians imprisoned in Israel. In the German rescue operation four of the Palestinians and all eleven Israeli hostages were killed. Three days later Israel launched attacks on Syria and Lebanon. There were reports that up to 500 people, many of them women and children, were killed in nine separate simultaneous Israeli air attacks (*Al-Nahar Arab Report*, 18 September 1972):

> The Phantoms and Skyhawks swooped on the suburban Damascus resort of al-Hama; the bombs fell indiscriminately on Palestinians in their hillside dwellings and on Syrians, in their cars or strolling by the river Barada on their weekend outing. Survivors recounted how they were machine-gunned as they ran for cover. (Hirst, 1977: 251)

In 1973 there were further hijackings by militant Arab groups. In that year Israel had also shot down a Libyan airliner that had strayed over the occupied Sinai peninsula, killing all 106 passengers. Later, Black September militants took over the Saudi Embassy in the Sudanese capital, demanding the release of Palestinian prisoners held in Jordanian jails. The authorities refused, and a Jordanian together with an American and a Belgian diplomat were killed. There followed, in quick succession, hijackings of Japanese, American and Dutch airliners. The worst loss of life occurred at Rome airport in December 1973 when Palestinian militants killed 34, mainly American, civilians. Eleven months later a British Airways VC10 was hijacked by the Martyr Abu Mahmud Group, who called on the British government to 'declare its responsibility for the greatest crime in history, which was the establishment of the [illegible]ist entity, and foreswear the accursed Balfour Declaration, w[illegible] brought tragedies and calamities to our region' (cited in

Hirst, 1977: 321–2). In the wake of this hijacking Yasser Arafat very publicly attempted to rein in the militants by arresting a number and amending the PLO criminal code to make hijacking that resulted in loss of life a capital offence.

The early 1970s had also seen the PLO begin to make diplomatic headway at the United Nations in its quest for institutional legitimacy and support for Palestinian nationalism. It received support at the UN from the Arab, non-aligned and newly decolonised states, which tended to vote as a block in support of Palestinian rights. In 1970 a General Assembly resolution was passed recognising the need for Palestinian self-determination. General Assembly Resolution 2649 'condemns those Governments that deny the right to self-determination of peoples recognised as being entitled to it, especially of the peoples of southern Africa and Palestine'. In 1974, UN Resolution 3246 was passed, which again stressed the need for Palestinian self-determination and added as a corollary that it was legitimate to 'struggle for liberation from colonial and foreign domination and alien subjugation by all available means, including armed struggle'. In November 1974, the UN adopted Resolution 3236, which established UN support for the creation of a Palestinian state: 'The General Assembly ... reaffirms the inalienable rights of the Palestinian people in Palestine, including (a) the right to self-determination without external interference (b) the right to national independence and sovereignty.'

Many Israelis, especially those on the political right, disputed the whole notion of Palestinian nationalism. They argued that it was a post-1967 invention created by the Arab states in order to wage a surrogate war against Israel. In 1969, the Israeli Prime Minister Golda Meir stated that 'It was not as though there was a Palestinian people in Palestine considering itself as a Palestinian people and we came and threw them out and took their country away from them. They did not exist' (*Sunday Times*, 15 June 1969, cited in Shlaim, 2000: 311). Similarly Netanyahu has argued that both Palestinian nationalism and Palestinian refugees are post-1967 fabrications:

> Indeed, most Palestinian Arabs have homes. Many of them, in fact, live as full citizens in Eastern Palestine – today called the Hashemite Kingdom of Jordan. Similarly, most of the Arabs of Judea-Samaria are not homeless refugees; they live in the same homes they occupied before the establishment of Israel. The number of actual refugees is close to nil. (2000: 156–8)

This view is disputed by multilateral bodies such as the United Nations, who have explicitly recognised in many resolutions the existence of a distinct Palestinian people, their rights to national self-determination, and the existence of over three and a half million refugees.

1973: THE OCTOBER WAR/THE YOM KIPPUR WAR

The War of Attrition had failed to secure the return of the occupied Sinai for Egypt but had instead left many of the Suez coastal cities devastated by Israeli raids. Shlaim claims that in the early 1970s Egypt made numerous attempts to regain the occupied Sinai through diplomacy but her peace overtures were rejected by Israel.[32] Shlaim suggests Israel's 'diplomacy of attrition' together with statements indicating that it intended to annex the Sinai left Sadat with no diplomatic option and made war inevitable.

On 6 October 1973, Egyptian and Syrian forces attacked Israeli troop concentrations in the occupied Sinai peninsula and Golan Heights. The Arab armies achieved early successes, with the Egyptian army crossing the Suez Canal and advancing into the Sinai, and the Syrian army forcing back the Israelis on the Golan Heights. Eventually the Israeli army turned the tables and regained the territorial losses it initially sustained. The war cost the lives of 2,832 Jews and 8,528 Arabs (Shlaim, 2000). There have been suggestions that the conflict nearly precipitated both a nuclear exchange between the superpowers and an Israeli nuclear strike on Egypt.[33]

The nature of the attack and the motivations of Syria and Egypt are contested. Netanyahu argues that the Arab forces had 'enormous advantages' over the Israelis, and the Israeli army had fought a 'pulverizing battle to keep the front from collapsing in the face of overwhelming numbers' (2000: 282). He claims that 'Israel's army was able, albeit by a hair's breadth, to prevent defeat in the face of a surprise attack' and that having 'so little to show for an onslaught stacked so decisively in their favour' was what brought Sadat to the negotiating table to sign a peace treaty with Israel at Camp David in 1979 (2000: 282). In contrast, Shlaim suggests that the Egyptian/ Syrian attack was a limited venture designed to bring Israel to the negotiating table and force a political settlement in which the lands captured in 1967 would be returned. In an exact reversal of Netanyahu's thesis, Finkelstein (2001) argues that it was Israel that finally agreed to come to the negotiating table at Camp David after Egypt and Syria demonstrated that they possessed a 'military option'.

Following the Yom Kippur War the Arab world led by Saudi Arabia instituted an oil embargo on the West, leading to a sharp rise in oil prices, which it is argued precipitated a major global recession. This again had the effect of focusing international attention on the need to resolve the conflict, or at least to neutralise some of its more dangerous elements.

CONFLICT IN LEBANON

Having been forced out of Jordan in 1970, the PLO relocated to Lebanon from where it fought a guerrilla war against the Israeli state, attacking both military and civilian targets. Sachar (1977) lists numerous deadly attacks by Palestinian infiltrators on Israelis and argues that during the mid-1970s the 'violence continued almost without respite' (1977: 810). Netanyahu notes that the PLO were using Lebanon as a base from which to fire Katyusha missiles across the border into Israel, which he maintains had a very damaging effect on the lives of those in Israel's northern towns and villages:

> The PLO used the territory of its de facto state to shell Israeli cities and towns. For years, the entire population of the northern border towns and villages were regularly driven into underground bomb shelters by barrages of PLO launched Katyusha missiles, the little brothers of the Scud missiles that

Iraq launched against Israel in 1991. By 1982, the population levels of Kiryat Shemona and Nahariya had fallen ominously; factories, schools and beaches were being closed repeatedly to avoid mass casualties during the shellings; and fear of economic ruin and depopulation had spread. (2000: 218–19)

During this period Israel bombed PLO positions, Lebanese villages and Palestinian refugee camps. The Israeli military analyst Ze'ev Schiff justified attacks on civilians on the basis that guerrillas used the villages and refugee camps for shelter:

In south Lebanon we struck the civilian population consciously because they deserved it ... the importance of [Mordechai] Gur's [Israeli chief of staff] remarks is the admission that the Israeli army has always struck civilian populations, purposely and consciously ... the army, he said, has never distinguished civilian [from military] targets ... [but] purposely attacked civilian targets even when Israeli settlements had not been struck. (*Ha'aretz*, 15 May 1978, cited in Chomsky, 1999: 181)

Israeli Foreign Minister Abba Eban argued that 'there was a rational prospect ultimately fulfilled that affected populations would exert pressure for the cessation of hostilities' (*Jerusalem Post*, 16 August 1981, cited in Chomsky, 1999: 182). The Lebanese villagers, however, were unarmed and in practice could do little to stop the armed guerrillas. The Lebanese army was too weak to remove the Palestinians, who had virtually formed a state-within-a-state. Official government casualty statistics suggest that the scale of Israeli raids was disproportionate to the Palestinian attacks. The Israeli authorities estimated that 106 Israeli civilians were killed by Palestinian guerrillas on Israel's northern border in the period between 1967 and 1982, at a rate of approximately seven a year (*Ha'aretz*, 22 June 1982, cited in Chomsky, 1999: 74). The American journalist Judith Coburn reported that diplomats in Beirut and UN officials estimated 3,500 Lebanese citizens were killed between 1967 and 1975, and at least twice as many Palestinian civilians, giving a rate of more than a thousand per year. Touring Southern Lebanon in the mid-1970s, Coburn found many villages 'attacked almost daily in recent months ... by airplane, artillery, tanks and gunboats', with the Israelis employing 'shells, bombs, phosphorous, incendiary bombs, CBUs [cluster bombs] and napalm' against Lebanese villages and refugee camps as part of what she claimed was a 'scorched earth' policy to remove the population and create a demilitarised zone (*New York Times*, 7 March 1975, cited in Chomsky, 1999: 190). By 1977 it was estimated that 300,000 Lebanese Muslims had been turned into refugees by the Israeli attacks (*New York Times*, 2 October 1977, cited in Chomsky, 1999: 191).

The PLO continued its diplomatic offensive at the United Nations. In November 1974, the UN officially granted the PLO observer status. Later that month Yasser Arafat addressed the UN General Assembly for the first time, giving his 'gun and olive branch' address. The leadership of the PLO argued for the ending of the armed struggle, in return for the creation of a mini-Palestinian state in the West Bank and Gaza Strip and a settlement of the refugee issue. This move was not accepted by all factions within the organisation, the PFLP leading the rejectionist wing, which was against the concept of the mini-state and the recognition of Israel. These moves did not impress the Israelis. Israel's foreign minister claimed that 'the voice of Arafat was, and remains the voice of indiscriminate terror, the voice of the gun, with nothing in it of the olive branch of peace' (cited in Hirst, 1977: 335). The call for the creation of a Palestinian mini-state between Israel and Jordan was similarly dismissed as a platform from which the PLO would attempt to destroy Israel. The Israeli daily *Yediot Aharonot* argued that 'no reasonable person ... can ask us to hand over these regions to the PLO, unless it expects Israel to commit suicide' (14 November 1974, cited in Hirst, 1977: 336).

In the mid-1970s both sides as well as Syria became involved in the Lebanese civil war. The 1943 power-sharing National Pact broke down in the mid-1970s, culminating in the all-out civil war of 1975–76. The conflict broadly concerned two rival groupings: first, the right-wing Christian-Maronite-Phalangist alliance, backed by Israel, which was economically dominant in the country, and second, the predominantly poor majority, which consisted of leftist Muslim-Lebanese and Palestinian groupings. In mid-1976, with the leftist Muslim coalition gaining the upper hand in the conflict, the Syrians intervened on the side of the Christians, occupying most of Lebanon apart from a southern strip bordering Israel. The intervention of the Syrian army at the behest of the Christians (and with the tacit support of Israel) brought a truce and relative calm to all but Southern Lebanon. The 18 months of civil war had devastated Beirut, which became partitioned, and killed tens of thousands of Palestinians and Lebanese. In April 1976, Israel and Syria reached a secret agreement with American mediation, splitting the area into 'spheres of influence'. Syria agreed to keep its troops north of the Litani River and not to install surface-to-air missiles there, recognising Southern Lebanon as Israel's security buffer.

In the mid-1970s, Israel began supplying the two major Christian Maronite militias, the Phalangists and Chamouns, with weapons. Jonathan Randal (1983), the former senior foreign correspondent of the *Washington Post*, suggests the conflict was strategically useful for Israel because it tied down two enemies, the Syrians and Palestinians, both of whom had come into conflict with the Christians by 1977. Israel was also backing General Haddad's South Lebanon Army (SLA), which was acting as its proxy force in South Lebanon. Randal (1983) notes that this was controversial because Haddad's forces had been involved in serious abuses including many instances of large-scale killings of civilians and were accused of involvement in the unlawful deaths of UN personnel. In 1978, Israel mounted a large-scale invasion of Southern Lebanon, claiming that it was in response to a Palestinian attack in Israel, which had left 37 Israelis and nine Palestinians dead.

The scale and effects of the invasion are disputed. Gilbert claims that 'several dozen PLO soldiers were killed or captured' and 'all PLO installations were systematically destroyed' (1999: 490). Randal claims it was civilians rather than guerrillas who bore the brunt of the attack:

> The destruction was on a scale well known in Vietnam. Aping the prodigal use of American firepower in Indo-China, the Israelis sought to keep their

> own casualties to a minimum – and succeeded. But they failed to wipe out the Palestinian commandos, who had plenty of time to scamper to safety north of the Litani River. Piling mattresses, clothes and families in taxis and overloaded pickup trucks, more than two hundred thousand Lebanese also fled north out of harm's way. They became exiles in their own country, squatters seizing unoccupied apartments, the source of yet more tension in West Beirut. The Israelis did succeed in massive killing: almost all the victims were Lebanese civilians – some one thousand according to the International Committee of the Red Cross. More than six thousand homes were badly damaged or destroyed. Half a dozen villages were all but levelled in a frenzy of violence in which Israeli troops committed atrocities. (1983: 209)

After three months under pressure from the United Nations, who condemned the attack, the IDF withdrew from Southern Lebanon and was replaced by a UN force. Most of the positions abandoned by the IDF were taken by the SLA. In January 1979, Ezer Weizman, the Israeli defence secretary, announced a controversial pre-emptive policy against Palestinian guerrillas in Southern Lebanon. He declared that Israel would not only strike in retaliation but 'at any time and any place that Israel deemed desirable' (cited in Randal, 1983: 220). In 1981 hostilities escalated in Lebanon. On 17 July Israel launched a major bombing raid on Southern Lebanon, hitting refugee camps, ports, Lebanon's main oil refinery and all but one of the bridges over the Litani and Zahrani rivers (Randal, 1983). The Israelis claimed that the raids were necessary to deal with a PLO arms build-up in Southern Lebanon. The Palestinians held fire for three days and then began shelling and rocketing northern Israel. On 17 July Israel bombed the Fakhani district in West Beirut, home to the PLO offices. More than 120 Palestinian and Lebanese civilians were killed, leading to international condemnation of the raid. The Palestinians then launched artillery attacks on 28 Israeli towns and settlements, damaging homes, crops and orchards, while tens of thousands of Israelis were temporarily forced to flee their homes in northern Israel (Randal, 1983). In the wake of this exchange both sides agreed to an American-brokered ceasefire.

DIPLOMACY AND THE CAMP DAVID ACCORDS

During this period, a number of attempts had been made by the Palestinians to push for a peace settlement. Palestinian representatives put forward a United Nations Security Council resolution in January 1976, which called for a two-state solution based on the 1967 borders, 'with appropriate arrangements ... to guarantee ... the sovereignty, territorial integrity and political independence of all states in the area and their right to live in peace within secure and recognised boundaries' (UN Security Council Resolution S/11940). The resolution received nine votes in favour, including France and the Soviet Union, but was blocked by a single vote against from the United States. Chomsky (1999) points to PLO acceptance of the Soviet–American peace plan of October 1977, the Soviet peace plan of 1981 and the Saudi 1982 peace plan as well as a number of public statements by PLO representatives in the late 1970s that the Palestinians were proposing to end the armed struggle in exchange for the creation of a mini-state in Gaza and the West Bank.[34] He notes that all such overtures were rejected by Israel. But some Israelis such as Binyamin Netanyahu have dismissed all such Palestinian peace overtures. These are seen as part of an attempt to force Israel to accept a PLO 'Trojan horse', whose purpose is to destroy the Israeli state. Netanyahu argues that after the 1973 War the Palestinians realised that they couldn't destroy Israel with a 'frontal military assault' but were planning 'an interim phase in which Israel would be reduced to dimensions that made it more convenient for the coup de grace'. This would be achieved in two phases: 'first create a Palestinian state on any territory vacated by Israel', and 'second mobilize from that state a general Arab military assault to destroy a shrunken and indefensible Israel' (2000: 239). Netanyahu claims that the Arabs have been deceiving the Western nations with a moderate front:

For the PLO is a Pan-Arab Trojan Horse, a gift that the Arabs have been trying to coax the Arabs into accepting for over twenty years, so that the West in turn can force Israel to let it in at the gates. The Arabs paint their gift up prettily with legitimacy with the pathos of its plight, with expressions for the cherished ideas of freedom, justice, and peace. Yet no matter how it is dressed up to conceal the fact, the ultimate aim of the gift remains: to be allowed within Israel's defensive wall, to be parked on the hills overlooking Tel-Aviv, where it can perform its grisly task. Every inch of Western acceptance – the cover stories, the banquets, the observer status, the embassies, and any territory the PLO has been able to get its hands on – it uses to push ever closer to its goal. (2000: 256)

In March 1978, 350 Israeli reservists sent a letter to Prime Minister Begin that accused the government of preferring to build settlements and create a 'Greater Israel' rather than make peace with the Arab world. This was partly in response to Begin's decision to support the creation of a number of new Gush Emunim settlements deep in the occupied territories. The letter marked the creation of the 'Peace Now' movement, which in September 1978 organised a mass rally of 100,000 Israelis in Tel-Aviv, the largest political demonstration in the state's history. The European Economic Community also pushed for a solution to the conflict during 1979. Leaders of the EEC meeting in Venice in June issued statements supportive of Palestinian statehood, and the president-elect of the European Commission, Gaston Thorn, travelled to the Middle East and met Yasser Arafat. The PLO was recognised by Ireland and Austria, while French President Giscard d'Estaing recommended the group be accepted as a partner in peace negotiations. The Europeans also attempted to widen Resolution 242 to include Palestinian self-determination. Ovendale (1999) claims that the United States made it clear that it would veto any European resolution in the Security Council that supported Palestinian rights.

In March 1979, Israel signed a peace agreement with Egypt in Washington, on terms very similar to the ones rejected by Israel in 1972. The progress to the final settlement had been long and tortuous, involving diplomacy stretching over several continents and many years. Israel agreed to hand back the Sinai peninsula in exchange for a comprehensive peace treaty, and demilitarisation of most of the Sinai. Both parties had compromised. Israel agreed to remove the settlements and airfields. Egypt dropped the issue of Jerusalem, and the two sides agreed on only a vague autonomy plan for the Palestinians, which would be implemented in stages over a number of years. The two signatories were subject to a great deal of criticism over the conclusion of the peace treaty. Begin was attacked by the right and religious parties for returning the Sinai. Sadat was criticised for breaking Arab unity by signing a peace treaty with Israel, without having achieved a deal on the key issues of Jerusalem, Palestinian statehood or a full Israeli withdrawal from Arab territory. Finkelstein (2001) suggests that the Israeli government agreed to peace with Egypt because it would neutralise the most powerful Arab military force threatening it, and subsequently allow it to break the core of the Palestinian national movement in Lebanon.

On 30 July 1980, the Israeli government formally annexed all of Jerusalem, and the following year the Golan Heights were annexed in violation of the Israel–Egypt peace agreement and Resolution 242. Both annexations drew immediate condemnation from the UN Security Council (Resolutions 478 and 497), which declared them to be illegal, and demanded their reversal. The plans for Palestinian autonomy were not developed, and Shlaim suggests that the Begin administration deliberately sabotaged the autonomy negotiations and expanded expropriations of Palestinian land and settlement-building, because it wanted to retain control over the West Bank and Gaza Strip:

> Begin managed the autonomy talks in such a way that nothing could possibly be achieved. The first sign was Begin's appointment of Dr Yosef Burg, the minister of the interior, to head Israel's six-man negotiating team. Burg was the leader of the National Religious Party, which saw Israel's right to Judea and Samaria as embedded in Scripture and supported the settlement activities of Gush Emunim. (2000: 381–2)

1982: THE INVASION OF LEBANON

On 6 June 1982, Israel invaded Lebanon and attacked PLO forces. It also engaged the Syrian army in its drive towards Beirut. In the early days of the conflict the *Economist* correspondent G.H. Jansen reported that the Israeli policy was to surround towns and cities 'so swiftly that civilian inhabitants were trapped inside, and then to pound them from land, sea and air. After a couple of days there would be a timid probing attack: if there was resistance the pounding would resume' (*Middle East International*, 2 July 1982, cited in Chomsky, 1999: 219). By the time an American-sponsored ceasefire came into effect on 11 June the Israeli army had reached the southern outskirts of Beirut. Shlaim (2000) suggests that Israel was expecting its Christian allies in Lebanon, led by Bashir Gemayel, to attack the PLO forces, who by this time were trapped in West Beirut. However, Gemayel was reluctant to take on the Palestinians and the Israelis did not want to get involved in potentially costly street fighting. By 13 June the Israelis had surrounded Beirut, and for the next two months they laid siege to the city and bombarded it with heavy weaponry.

The Israeli commander, Ariel Sharon, who led the Israeli attack, claimed that 'no army in the history of modern warfare ever took such pains to prevent civilian casualties as did the Israeli Defence Forces' and that the 'Jewish doctrine' of *tohar haneshek* (purity of arms) was adhered to 'scrupulously', with the Israeli army 'attacking only predetermined PLO positions and in bombing and shelling buildings only when they served as PLO strongholds' (*New York Times*, 29 August 1982, cited in Chomsky, 1999: 243–4). Gilbert (1999) also stressed that the Israelis concentrated their attacks on PLO strongholds, although he notes that on one occasion a hospital was seriously damaged. Other reports from journalists in Beirut suggested that the Israelis were bombing civilian areas indiscriminately. The *Independent* journalist Robert Fisk wrote that the Israelis were employing 'time-on target salvoes', which 'laid 50 shells at a time' across residential areas, 'slaughtering everyone within a 500 yard radius of the explosions' (2001: 284). He also reported that the Israelis used cluster bombs, and phosphorous bombs, which were designed to create fires and cause untreatable burns. The Israeli daily *Ha'aretz* also noted the use of vacuum bombs, which ignite aviation fuel in such a way as to create immense pressure and implode large buildings. These were reportedly dropped on residential areas (11 August 1982). A Canadian surgeon, Chris Giannou, who had been working in a Palestinian hospital, testified before the US Congress that he had witnessed the 'total, utter devastation of residential areas, and the blind, savage, indiscriminate destruction of refugee camps by simultaneous shelling and carpet bombing from aircraft, gunboats, tanks and artillery'. He testified that cluster bombs and phosphorous bombs had been used widely in residential areas and that he had seen 'savage and indiscriminate beatings' of prisoners, which were sometimes fatal as well as frequent use of torture.[35]

The bombing intensified during July and August, and Hirsh Goodman reported that it continued, even after an agreement had been reached in principle for the PLO to leave (*Jerusalem Post*, 1 October 1982, cited in Chomsky, 1999: 241). In July, Yitzak Rabin ordered all supplies of food, water, medicines and fuel to be cut from the city. By 4 August Elaine Carey reported that eight of the nine orphanages in Beirut had been destroyed by cluster and phosphorous bombs, despite clear markings and Israeli assurances that they would be spared (*Christian Science Monitor*, 4 August 1982, cited in Chomsky, 1999: 225). On 12 August the bombing reached a peak. The American journalist Charles Powers wrote that:

> To many the siege of Beirut seemed gratuitous brutality ... The arsenal of weapons unleashed in a way that has not been seen since the Vietnam war, clearly horrified those who saw the results firsthand and through film and news reports at a distance. The use of cluster bombs and white phosphorous shells, a vicious weapon was widespread ... In the last hours of the last air attack on Beirut, Israeli planes carpet bombed Borg el Brajne [a refugee camp]. There were no fighting men left there only the damaged homes of Palestinian families, who once again would have to leave and find another place to live. (*Los Angeles Times*, 29 August 1982, cited in Chomsky, 1999: 242)

Eventually at the end of August the PLO forces were evacuated from Beirut to Tunis. Outside Beirut there were reports of widespread destruction of refugee camps and

Lebanese villages. In Sidon, Fisk noted that over 2,000 Lebanese civilians were killed in air attacks, which he described as 'the most ferocious ever delivered upon a Lebanese city' (2001: 204). The head of the UN refugee agency that administered the camps, Olof Rydbeck, said that 32 years of work had been 'wiped out', with 'practically all of the schools, clinics and installations of the agency in ruins' (*New York Times*, 19 August 1982, cited in Chomsky, 1999: 223). The scale of civilian and PLO casualties during the war is contested. Gilbert (1999) claims that 460 Lebanese civilians and 6,000 PLO fighters were killed. The Lebanese police estimated 19,085 killed through to August, with 6,775 killed in Beirut, 84 per cent of whom were civilians (*Christian Science Monitor*, 21 December 1982, cited in Chomsky, 1999: 221). The United Nations estimated 13,500 houses severely damaged in West Beirut, thousands more in other parts of the country, not taking into account damage to the refugee camps, which were towns themselves (*Christian Science Monitor*, 18 November 1982, cited in Chomsky, 1999: 223). There were also reports that large numbers of teenage and adult Lebanese and Palestinian males were taken to camps where they were humiliated and tortured.[36]

Chomsky cites testimony from the IDF Lieutenant Colonel Dov Yirmiah, which appeared in the Israeli daily *Yediot Ahronot* on the fate of Palestinian and Lebanese detainees:

> He tells story after story of prisoners savagely and endlessly beaten in captivity, of torture and humiliation of prisoners, and of the many who died of beatings and thirst in Israeli prisons or concentration camps in Lebanon .... The long and repeated interrogations were accompanied by constant beatings, or attacks by dogs on leashes, or the use of air rifles that cause intense pain but do not kill ... New loads of clubs had to be brought into the camps to replace those broken under interrogation. The torturers were 'experts in their work,' the prisoners report, and knew how to make blows most painful, including blows to the genitals, until the prisoners confessed that they were 'terrorists'. (8 November 1982, cited in Chomsky, 1999: 240)

Other reports in the Israeli press claimed that members of Israel's proxy militia, the South Lebanon Army, were allowed in the camps to torture prisoners and that some gang-raped women and attempted to force them to have sex with dogs (*Koteret Rashit*, 16 March 1983, cited in Chomsky, 1999: 236). After the PLO had agreed to leave Lebanon one of the war's most notorious incidents occurred at the refugee camps at Shatila and Sabra. After the departure of the PLO from Lebanon, the Israeli forces sealed off these camps on 16 September and allowed in between 100 and 130 Phalangist and Haddadist troops. Ariel Sharon claimed that the camps contained 2,000 well-armed Palestinian fighters and that the Christian forces had been sent in to clear them out. However, Edward Walsh argues that 'no one has publicly explained how the Israelis expected 100 to 130 Phalangists to defeat such a force of Palestinians' (*Washington Post*, 26 December 1982, cited in Chomsky, 1999: 369), and in a visit to the camp a few days before the killings journalists reported finding no military presence (*Time*, 4 October 1982).

Once in the camps the Phalangist forces raped and killed many of the camps inhabitants, who were primarily women, children and the elderly. The death toll is disputed. The official Israeli Kahan Commission estimated 700–800 killed, the Lebanese authorities put the figure at approximately 2,000, while the Israeli journalist Amnon Kapeliouk (1984), citing evidence from the International Committee of the Red Cross, estimated 3,000–3,500. Responsibility for the killings has also been partly attributed to the United States, who gave explicit assurances that the Muslim civilian population of West Beirut would be protected as part of the PLO deal to evacuate Beirut (Ovendale, 1999). The massacres were condemned by the United Nations by 147 votes to two (Israel, United States), and international lawyers in Belgium have since attempted to indict the Israeli commanders Ariel Sharon and Amos Yaron for war crimes.

The Lebanon War appeared to split Israeli society. Some questioned whether the scale of death and destruction inflicted on Southern Lebanon was proportionate to the threat posed by Palestinian militants. In 1983 a debate on Zionism was held at Tel-Aviv University in which Aluf Hareven of the Van Leer Institute commented:

> According to the figures provided by the Ministry of the Interior Yosef Burg, in 1980, 10 Jews were killed by terrorists and in 1981–8. In contrast we have killed about a thousand terrorists in 1982, and caused the loss of life of thousands of inhabitants of an enemy country. If so, it results that for every 6–8 Jews sacrificed, we kill in return thousands of Gentiles. This is undoubtedly, a spectacular situation, an uncommon success of Zionism. I might even dare to say – exaggerated. (*Migvan*, October/November 1982, cited in Chomsky, 1999: 74)

The massacres at Sabra and Shatila also led to the largest protests in Israel's history. On 25 September 1982 more than 400,000 Israelis joined a Peace Now demonstration in Tel-Aviv. Others suggested that a large part of the population was unconcerned if not approving of the events at the refugee camps:

> In the matter of Sabra and Shatila – a large part of the community, perhaps the majority, is not at all troubled by the massacre itself. Killing of Arabs in general, and Palestinians in particular, is quite popular, or at least 'doesn't bother anyone' in the words of youth these days. Ever since the massacre I have been surprised to hear from educated, enlightened people, 'the conscience of Tel Aviv', the view that the massacre itself, as a step towards removing the remaining Palestinians from Lebanon is not terrible. It is just too bad that we were in the neighbourhood. (*Ha'aretz*, 19 November 1982, cited in Chomsky, 1999: 395)

Israel's motives for launching the attack are contested. Mitchell Bard (2003), the director of the American-Israeli Cooperative Institute, points to three reasons for Israel's decision to attack Lebanon. Firstly, he claims that the PLO was repeatedly breaching the ceasefire negotiated by the Americans in July 1981 and attacking Israelis across the Lebanese border. Secondly, he alleges that 15,000–18,000 PLO members were encamped in Southern Lebanon and were equipping themselves with a huge arsenal, including rockets, surface-to-air missiles, mortars, tanks and enough weapons to arm five brigades. He suggests that Israeli strikes and commando raids could not prevent the emergence of this 'PLO army'. Finally, Bard points to the attempt on the life of the Israeli ambassador to London, Shlomo Argov, by the Abu Nidal group. All of these explanations have been disputed.[37] Shlaim suggests that Israel had two objectives: (1) to create a new political order in Lebanon; and (2) to 'destroy the PLO's military infrastructure in Lebanon and undermine it as a political organisation' (2000: 396). Former IDF education officer Mordechai Bar-on argued that 'there is no doubt that the [war's] central aim was to deal a crushing blow to the national aspirations of the Palestinians and to their very existence as a nation endeavouring to define itself and gain the right to self-determination' (*New Outlook*, October 1982, cited in Chomsky, 1999: 203). With the PLO infrastructure destroyed and the refugees dispersed, some commentators suggested that the organisation might revert to hijacking and therefore undermine its growing political status:

> If the PLO were now thrown out of Lebanon – or, better yet, reduced to mad dog terrorism that would destroy its growing political and diplomatic legitimacy – then Israel stood a better chance of annexing the West Bank and Gaza Strip still thoroughly loyal to Arafat's leadership despite his many errors. (Randal, 1983: 250)

Shlaim (2000) suggests that another aspect of Sharon's 'big plan' was to install Israel's Christian ally Bashir Gemayel in power in Lebanon, and force the Palestinian refugees out of Lebanon to Jordan, leading to the overthrow of the Hashemite monarchy and its conversion to a Palestinian state. This would weaken international pressure on Israel to vacate the West Bank and allowing Israel to annex this territory. Neither of the suggested geostrategic aims were achieved. Bashir Gemayel was assassinated shortly after the war while the Hashemite monarchy remained intact in Jordan.

In the aftermath of the Sabra and Shatila killings, American marines returned to Lebanon as part of a multinational force. They, however, soon came into conflict with Shia and Druze forces opposed to Israel's occupation of Southern Lebanon.

When US warships shelled Druze positions, it appeared that the US had entered the civil war in support of the Christian–Israeli alliance. On 23 October, a suicide bomber killed 256 American and 58 French troops in Lebanon, leading to the withdrawal of American and European forces. A Shiite group with links to Iran later claimed responsibility for the attack. Ovendale (1999) claims that after the 1982 War Israel and the US strengthened their political and military ties by embarking on joint weapons projects. In 1986, the Israeli nuclear technician Mordechai Vanunu revealed in the *Sunday Times* the existence of Israel's substantial nuclear weapons capability. He was subsequently drugged and kidnapped in Rome by the Israeli secret service. After being taken back to Israel he received an 18-year prison term. Recent newspaper reports suggest that the Israeli nuclear arsenal has increased to approximately 200 warheads, many of which are fitted to American-supplied Harpoon cruise missiles capable of hitting any of Israel's Arab neighbours (*Observer*, 12 October 2003).

In the mid-1980s further attempts were also made to find a negotiated solution to the conflict. In February 1985, Yasser Arafat and King Hussein of Jordan issued the Amman Declaration, which proposed Palestinian self-determination within a Palestinian–Jordanian confederation. The composition of the negotiating team proved a problem, with Israel refusing to negotiate with any PLO members. Margaret Thatcher attempted to push the plan and proposed a peace conference to include PLO members. However, the plans were derailed by a series of events. Firstly, Abu Nidal, backed by Syria, threatened to assassinate any PLO members who accepted Thatcher's invitation. Then, on 25 September 1985, three Israelis were killed on a boat in Larnaca. The Israeli government blamed the PLO. The PLO claimed the three were Mossad agents. Israel then dispatched a number of American-made F-16 fighters to bomb the PLO headquarters in Tunis. In the attack, 58 Palestinians and 15 Tunisians were killed. The attack was supported by the US but condemned by the European Community and the United Nations. Soon afterwards a small Palestinian group, the Palestine Liberation Front, hijacked the liner *Achille Lauro* and killed an elderly disabled Jewish passenger before surrendering. Following the hijacking the US pressurised Britain to cancel a scheduled meeting between the Foreign Secretary and PLO members. Britain then insisted that the PLO members sign a statement denouncing all forms of political violence. They refused, arguing that this would cover armed resistance to the Israeli occupation of the West Bank and Gaza Strip. The meeting was then cancelled. Soon afterwards King Hussein of Jordan announced the end of his collaboration with the PLO leadership, blaming Arafat's refusal to accept Resolutions 242 and 338. In the wake of this rupture between the PLO and Jordan, King Hussein and Shimon Peres kept close diplomatic links and considered ways of restarting peace talks while excluding any members of the PLO from negotiations (Shlaim, 2000). Israel's pursuance of the 'Jordanian option', Shlaim suggests, was blocked by the Israeli premier Yitzak Shamir who was opposed to any international conference that might involve pressure from outside mediators.

1987: THE FIRST INTIFADA

On 9 December 1987, following the death of four Gazans in a road traffic incident, Palestinians from the Jebalya refugee camp began throwing stones at an Israeli army compound. Within days unrest spread to the West Bank. Unarmed Palestinian men, women and children attacked Israeli soldiers and armoured personnel carriers. Benny Morris notes that the intifada was 'not an armed rebellion but a massive, persistent campaign of civil resistance, with strikes and commercial shutdowns accompanied by violent (though unarmed) demonstrations against the occupying forces' (1992: 561). The intifada lasted six years until it was called off by the Palestinian leadership in the wake of the Oslo agreements. The factors behind it are contested. Netanyahu has argued that the Israeli administration in the occupied territories had instituted a 'liberal policy aimed at radically improving the lives of the Palestinians' and that material and educational prosperity had gone hand in hand with political rights, including 'a press consisting of newspapers representing various factions (some openly sympathetic to the PLO) and the right to directly appeal all decisions to the democratic court system' (2000: 176). He maintains that the impetus for the intifada was 'virulent PLO agitation', which led the population in the occupied territories to adopt 'ever more extreme and implacable positions' (2000: 177). He also claims that the PLO had forced children out of their schools to take part in confrontations with Israeli forces. Gilbert blames Jordan for not integrating the Palestinians living in the West Bank into Jordanian society before 1967, and argues that the impetus for the intifada came from a 'bitter hard core of extremists who were prepared to face Israeli bullets in order to defy the occupiers and assert their national identity' (1999: 525). Some Israelis blamed outside agitation for the intifada. Yitzak Rabin accused Iran and Syria of fomenting unrest. Others have questioned whether Israeli policy in the occupied territories was really liberal and suggest that the intifada was the result of severe and persistent human rights abuses. This is made clear in a report by the Israeli Committee for Solidarity with Bir Zeit (the West Bank University periodically closed by the Israeli authorities). It described the Israeli administration in the occupied territories as an 'attempt to revive an old well-known colonial method in a new "original" Israeli form' in order to create 'an Israeli Bantustan, which imposes on the Palestinians the role of hewers of wood and drawers of water for Israeli society'. To achieve this, the report suggested that there was widespread and violent suppression of all forms of political activity, and that 'quislings from the Village Leagues' together with settler groups inflicted 'humiliation, harassment and terror' on the local population.[38] The United Nations also produced a number of reports in the mid-1980s that were critical of Israeli human rights abuses in the occupied territories and pointed to widespread acts of violence committed against Palestinians by armed settlers.[39] Israel Shahak argues that such abuses were the main factor behind the intifada and cites examples from the Israeli press:

In fact, before the intifada, the daily oppression, humiliations, land confiscations and arbitrariness of the Israeli regime were steadily increasing. This increase, duly recorded by the Hebrew press, was the chief reason for the outbreak of the intifada. Readers of Israel's Hebrew-language press are aware of how outrageously the Israeli armed forces were behaving before the intifada. On June 19, 1987, Eyal Ehrlich reported in an article in *Ha'aretz* headlined, 'An occupier against his will,' the testimony of a young Israeli soldier assigned to serve in the border guards. Whenever a Palestinian is accosted to show his I.D., the soldier wrote, its checking is always accompanied by 'a slap, a punch, a kick.' 'The border guards usually enjoy beating the Arabs,' the account continues. 'They derive pleasure from it ... Sometimes I feel like a Nazi when I watch my friends in action. I try hard to stay away from one of my commanders ... He always behaves very badly toward the locals: with violence, beatings, and the like ... The soldiers spit in the faces of the Arabs, or they kick them in the testicles. And there is always that slap in the face.' An article in *Hadashot* of July 7, 1987 by Menahem Shizaf was headlined, 'Border guards order the Arabs to masturbate and to lick the floor.' It described the treatment meted out to Palestinian workers from the occupied territories who were found spending the night in shacks in Israel rather than returning to their homes. (*Washington Report on Middle East Affairs*, March 1991)

The Israeli minister of defence Yitzak Rabin explained that the Israeli response to the intifada would consist of 'force, might, beatings' (*New York Times*, 23 January 1988, cited in the *New York Review of Books*, 17 March 1988), while Prime Minister Shamir was reported in the Israeli publication *Hadashot* as warning those protesting against the occupation that they would be crushed 'like grasshoppers' with their heads 'smashed against the boulders and walls' and that 'we say to them from the heights of this mountain and from the perspective of thousands of years of history that they are like grasshoppers compared to us' (6 January 1988, cited in Chomsky, 1999: 482). By February 1988 the intifada became formalised with the establishment of the United National Leadership of the Uprising. The organisation encouraged strikes among those who worked in Israel and attacks on the Israeli administrative structure. Taxes were withheld, those who worked as administrators and tax collectors resigned and Israeli goods were boycotted (Ovendale, 1999). Roadblocks were set up to keep out the Israeli army, and Palestinians tried to create an alternative system of local self-government independent of the military authority.

In February 1988, the United States attempted to put forward a peace plan based on Palestinian autonomy in the occupied territories. The plan was rejected by Israel and the PLO, who noted that it made no mention of statehood. In April, Abu Jihad, the PLO second-in-command, was assassinated by Israel in Tunis. The Tunisian government complained to the UN Security Council. The Israeli daily *Ma'ariv* later reported that the future prime minister Ehud Barak had directed the assassination from a navy ship off Tunis (4 July 1988). In July, King Hussein of Jordan announced that his country was severing its links with the West Bank, effectively killing the 'Jordanian option' that had long been favoured by the US and some Israeli leaders. In September, Yasser Arafat told the European Parliament in Strasbourg that the PLO would accept Israel's right to security if Israel recognised a Palestinian mini-state. In November the Palestinian National Council meeting in Algiers agreed to recognise Israel, as well as all UN resolutions dating back to 1947 and to foreswear its claim to all of mandatory Palestine. It also proclaimed the establishment of the state of Palestine with East Jerusalem as its capital. The Israeli prime minister, Shamir, dismissed the resolutions as a 'deceptive propaganda exercise, intended to create the impression of moderation and of achievements for those carrying out violent acts in the territories of Judea and Samaria' (cited in Shlaim, 2000: 466). Yasser Arafat wanted to appeal to the UN General Assembly, but despite being recognised by more than sixty nations the United States refused him an entry visa (Ovendale, 1999). The General Assembly then voted to hold its plenary session in Geneva. Arafat, under strong pressure from the American secretary of state George Shultz, announced that the PLO accepted Resolutions 242 and 338, as well as Israel's right to exist, and renounced 'terrorism'.

Meanwhile Israel's response to the intifada was attracting widespread international criticism. By January 1989 the US

State Department reported that the unrest had claimed the lives of eleven Israelis and 366 Palestinians. Some on the Israeli right argued that the criticism of Israel and media coverage of the intifada was biased and unfair, and that the Israeli response was restrained and proportionate. Netanyahu, for instance, commented that:

> Ignoring the Arab reign of terror in the Palestinian streets, the media created for themselves nightly instalments of a popular romance drama: heroic underdog in search of self-determination taking on a terrifying Israeli tyrant ... Since viewers were being told this was an 'army of occupation' – that is, it had no right to be there in the first place – the media managed to transform even the most necessary aspects of maintaining law and order into unforgivable crimes. Utterly lost from the images on the screen was the organised nature of the rioting, the internecine violence, and the terrorised lives of the innocent Arabs (and Jews) who were ground under the intifada's heel. Similarly lost were the restrictive firing orders that stayed the hand of every Israeli soldier, and the swift trial of the 208 Israelis who in any way disobeyed these orders – as against the tens of thousands of Israeli soldiers and reservists who followed the regulations with impeccable restraint. (2000: 181–2)

The United Nations, NGOs, human rights groups and some Israeli soldiers disputed this. In December 1988, the UN General Assembly passed a resolution by 106 to 2 (Israel, United States), which condemned the conduct of the IDF and settlers during the intifada. The resolution 'declare[d] once more that Israel's grave breaches of that Convention are war crimes and an affront to humanity'. Among many criticisms the resolution 'strongly condemned' the 'implementation of an "iron-fist" policy against the Palestinian people ... the escalation of Israeli brutality since the beginning of the uprising ... the ill-treatment and torture of children and minors under detention and/or imprisonment ... the killing and wounding of defenceless demonstrators ... the breaking of bones and limbs of thousands of civilians ... the usage of toxic gas, which resulted, inter alia, in the killing of many Palestinians' (United Nations, 1988). Israel was particularly criticised for its treatment of children during the intifada. A thousand-page study from

Save the Children documented the 'indiscriminate beating, tear-gassing, and shooting of children'. The report found that the average age of the victims was ten years old and that the majority of those who were shot were not participating in stone throwing. The report also alleged that in 80 per cent of cases where children were shot the Israeli army prevented the victims from receiving medical attention. The report concluded that more than 50,000 children required medical attention for injuries including gunshot wounds, tear gas inhalation and multiple fractures (report cited in Finkelstein, 1996: 47). The August 1989 bulletin from the Israeli League for Human and Civil Rights was entitled 'Deliberate Murder' and reported on the targeting of Palestinian children in leadership roles. It found that the Israeli army and snipers from 'special units' had 'carefully chosen' the children who were shot in the head or heart and died instantaneously (report cited in Finkelstein, 1996: 47). Other reports from Israeli human rights groups and articles in the Israeli press also allege that torture, including severe beating and electric shocks, was used extensively against detainees including children.[40]

The intifada also saw the birth of Hamas, the Islamic opposition movement formed by Sheik Yassin in February 1988. The organisation, which emerged out of the Muslim Brotherhood, stressed a return to conservative Islamic values and provided a network of health and social services for Palestinians in the occupied territories. For many years the organisation received extensive funding from Israel (Shlaim, 2000; Chomsky, 1999; Mishal & Sela, 2000). Shlaim claims that this was done 'in the hope of weakening the secular nationalism of the PLO' (2000: 459). Chomsky (1999) suggests such a weakening would be beneficial to Israel because it would allow them to evade a political solution to the conflict that might involve returning the occupied territories. The Hamas charter issued in August 1988 argued that all of Palestine belonged to the Muslim nation as a religious endowment and that it was each Muslim's duty to engage in jihad ('struggle') to 'liberate' Palestine. The degree to which its intentions match its rhetoric is disputed. Most Israelis regard the organisation as fundamentalist and uncompromising, dedicated to killing Jews and destroying the Israeli state. But two Israeli academics, Shaul Mishal and Avraham Sela, suggest that the organisation is more complex and pragmatic than this. They suggest that Hamas utilises 'controlled violence' as a 'means rather than an end' to mobilise political support and is 'cognizant of power relations and political feasibility' (2000: viii). They argue that its main purpose has been to establish itself as the major force in Palestinian political life and that in the future it 'may find it can accept a workable formula of co-existence with Israel in place of armed struggle' (2000: ix). In 1989, the group's founder Sheik Yassin was arrested by Israel, and in the occupied territories the Israelis increased their use of deportations and curfews in an attempt to suppress the intifada. They also outlawed the committees administering the uprising. This was a serious problem for Palestinians as they saw the committees as the nucleus of the self-governing institutions they hoped to build, once the occupation ended.

In 1989, Yitzak Shamir put forward an initiative that proposed elections and expanded Palestinian autonomy in exchange for the ending of the intifada. Shamir set down certain preconditions. They were that there would be no Palestinian state, no PLO involvement (even if its representatives triumphed in the elections) and no participation in the elections for the inhabitants of East Jerusalem. The plans were eventually derailed by members of Shamir's own cabinet, principally Ariel Sharon, David Levy and Yitzhak Moda'i, who argued that Israel was giving too much away, and was adopting too liberal an attitude to the intifada (Shlaim, 2000). Egypt and the United States then put forward their own peace initiatives. These precipitated a split in what was then a National Unity government in Israel, which led to its downfall. One part of the government, the Labour Alignment, unsuccessfully urged Shamir to accept the American initiative, while some members of the right-wing Likud party felt Israel was making too many concessions and not cracking down sufficiently hard on the intifada. For six weeks the Labor party's Shimon Peres tried unsuccessfully to form a new coalition; eventually Yitzak Shamir formed one in which his Likud party linked up with ultra-nationalist and religious parties. This new coalition, which Shlaim suggests was the most right wing and hard-line (in its attitudes to the Arabs) in Israel's history, immediately announced that it would end the intifada, create new settlements and expand existing ones (2000). It also insisted there would be no Palestinian state, no negotiation with the PLO and no sharing of Jerusalem.

The intifada, which continued to smoulder during this period, was reignited in October 1990 when Israeli troops killed 21 Palestinians on the Temple Mount in Jerusalem. The Israelis claimed they had responded to acts of stone throwing directed at Israeli worshippers. The Palestinians claimed that the stone throwing only began after the Israelis started shooting. The UN Security Council condemned the killings, but Israel managed to prevent the UN from acting on Palestinian demands to replace the Israeli military government in the occupied territories with a UN force (Ovendale, 1999).

In August 1990, the Iraq War intervened when Saddam Hussein invaded Kuwait and occupied the country. Five months later an American-led coalition attacked Iraq forcing its withdrawal from Kuwait. Both the Palestinians in the occupied territories and the PLO leadership allied itself with Saddam Hussein because of the Iraqi dictator's attempt to make a 'linkage' between Iraqi withdrawal from Kuwait and Israeli withdrawal from the occupied territories, and because he struck at the Israeli state with Scud missiles. In doing so the Palestinian leadership effectively lost much of the political capital it had built up over many years, while Israel benefited internationally by not responding to the Iraqi attacks. In the aftermath of the war the US moved to bring Israel and its Arab adversaries together in an international peace conference.

THE BEGINNING OF THE OSLO PROCESS

In Madrid at the end of October 1991 an Israeli delegation met Palestinian and other representatives from Israel's 'confrontation states' (Syria, Jordan, Lebanon). Although the Palestinian representatives were pro-PLO, they were not publicly stated as being members of the organisation, as to do so would have subjected them to imprisonment under Israeli law. The Americans who set up the conference insisted that it be based on UN Resolutions 242 and 338 and the principle of 'land for peace'. This premise was accepted by the Palestinians but rejected by the Israelis (Shlaim, 2000). In the run-up to the conference, the Likud administration announced a new wave of settlement-building designed to double the settler population in the occupied territories in four years. Little progress was made in negotiations, either in Madrid or in the five rounds of bilateral talks that took place in Washington. Shlaim argues that an 'immense gap' separated the parties:

> The Palestinians started with the assumption that they were a people with national rights and that the interim arrangements under discussion were the precursor to independence and should be shaped accordingly. The Israeli government started with the assumption that the Palestinians were the inhabitants of the territories with no national rights of any kind and certainly no rights to independence, not even after the end of the transitional period. (2000: 493)

In June 1992, the Israeli population went to the polls to elect a new administration. The Likud party pledged to continue the peace process while retaining all the occupied territories and expanding settlement-building. The Labor party vowed to conclude a deal on Palestinian autonomy, allow residents of East Jerusalem to take part in negotiations and freeze the construction of the 'political settlements' deep in the occupied territory. Labor won the election under Yitzak Rabin in a major political swing, which ended 15 years of Likud rule. In an Israeli newspaper interview just after his election defeat Shamir declared that 'I would have carried on autonomy talks for ten years, and meanwhile we would have reached half a million people in Judea and Samaria' (*Ma'ariv*, 26 June 1992).

Over the next 20 months Israelis and Palestinians engaged in ten rounds of negotiations in Washington that produced no tangible results. In the middle of those negotiations Rabin deported 416 Hamas activists to Lebanon following the killing of an Israeli border policeman. The deportations, which were condemned by the UN as a breach of international law, were intended to curb Hamas's influence but actually had the opposite effect. Mishal and Sela argue that they were a 'milestone in Hamas's decision to use car bombs and suicide attacks as a major modus operandi against Israel', because they came into contact with Hezbullah guerrillas who provided training in such techniques (2000: 65–6). They note that Hamas first used suicide attacks shortly after the return of the deportees to the occupied territories.[41]

THE DECLARATION OF PRINCIPLES

While the official negotiations continued, the Israelis decided to open up a second and secret channel of diplomacy in Oslo. For the first time they agreed to negotiate with a section of the PLO. These talks bypassed the bulk of the PLO and Fatah, with negotiations directed only towards Yasser Arafat and a few close associates. In September 1993, the Declaration of Principles between the Palestinians and Israel was finally brought into the open and signed by both parties on the White House lawn. The declaration was an agenda for negotiations that stipulated that within four months of signing the agreement Israel had to withdraw completely from Gaza and Jericho, with a Palestinian police force taking over internal security in those areas. Israel would still maintain overall responsibility for external security and foreign affairs. Elsewhere in the West Bank, Palestinians were to take control of five spheres: education, health, social welfare, direct taxation and tourism. Within nine months elections were to be held for a Palestinian Authority, which was to assume responsibilities for those municipal affairs. Final-status negotiations were scheduled to start within two years and were due to be completed within five years. All of the most serious issues affecting the two parties, including possible Palestinian statehood, borders, refugees, settlements and Jerusalem, were postponed to the final settlement talks. The PLO agreed to accept UN Resolutions 242 and 338, to end the armed struggle against Israel and amend the parts of the

Palestinian National Charter that called for the destruction of the Israeli state. Israel agreed to recognise the PLO as the representative of the Palestinian people. The Declaration of Principles brought an end to the first intifada which, according to the Israeli human rights group B'Tselem, had resulted in the deaths of 160 Israelis and 1,162 Palestinians (B'Tselem, 2003a).

The treaty met with opposition on both Israeli and Palestinian sides. Likud and the right-wing nationalist and religious parties denounced the agreement as a betrayal of the settlers in the occupied territories, an end to Biblical Greater Israel, and a mortal threat to the security of the state. They argued that the occupied territories could not be ceded by politicians as they had been eternally promised to the Jews by God. Binyamin Netanyahu, the Likud leader, completely rejected the accord and pledged to cancel it if he became prime minister. He compared the agreement to the appeasement of Hitler and told Peres, 'You are even worse than Chamberlain. He imperilled the safety of another people, but you are doing it to your own people' (cited in Shlaim, 2000: 521). The accord was eventually approved by the Knesset by a margin of 61 votes to 50. Israeli public opinion on the accords was generally favourable, with 65 per cent saying they approved of the agreement and only 13 per cent declaring themselves 'very much against' it (Shlaim, 2000).

In an analysis of Palestinian reaction to the Oslo Accords, Mouin Rabbani identified four distinct positions and argued that 'contrary to most press reports the fault line ... within the Palestinian body politic is not an ideological one separating peace-loving moderates from violent extremists' but rather one that revolves 'primarily around issues of substance and procedure' (*Middle East International*, 24 September 1993). He claimed that only a few Palestinians were 'enthusiastic supporters', while a majority whom he characterised as 'optimistic and desperate in equal measure' had serious doubts but were prepared to give the agreement a chance. He suggested that this large group could quickly turn against the agreement if the human rights situation did not improve, and the settlement activity and occupation continued. The third group he identified comprised senior political and cultural figures[42] such as Edward Said, who although supporting a peaceful resolution of the conflict, nevertheless regarded the accords as 'deeply flawed' and 'potentially fatal to Palestinian national aspirations'. They objected to Arafat signing the document without public debate or consultation and believed it was a bad deal. They pointed out the Palestinians were agreeing to end the intifada and renounce their rights to 78 per cent of historic Palestine without any guarantee of statehood or agreement to remove settlements (or even stop settlement-building). Neither were there any commitments to improve the human rights situation, or to resolve the refugee issue and status of Jerusalem. For this group, the agreement undermined the internationally recognised rights of Palestinians and 'foreshadows permanent dispossession of the majority of Palestinians' as well as creating the potential conditions for a civil war. The fourth position that Rabbani identifies is that of the rejectionists who comprise both the radical Islamic and secular movements such as Hamas and the PFLP, and their supporters in the occupied territories. These groups, argues Rabbani, regarded the agreement as a 'textbook case of Bantustanisation' in which the principal Palestinian weapon, the intifada, was being liquidated so that Palestinians could become the joint administrators of the occupation, in a weak subservient statelet or series of statelets. Rabbani suggests that had the agreement involved moves towards real statehood and been reached in 'conformity with the Palestinian national consensus and properly ratified' then much of the rejectionist camp would at least have tacitly accepted the deal – although the exceptions to this would still have included Islamic Jihad and some sections of Hamas.

The 1993 Declaration of Principles was followed in February 1994 by the signing of the new set of documents in Cairo. The IDF agreed to redeploy its forces from urban centres to rural areas, allowing it to maintain control of overall security and land crossings. On 25 February, Dr Baruch Goldstein, an American-born settler and member of the Kach party, opened fire with an IDF-issued Galil assault rifle on Muslim worshippers at the Tomb of the Patriarchs in Hebron, killing 29 people before he himself was killed. Rachelle Marshall, a journalist and member of the Jewish Peace Union, writes that the killings were followed by a five-week round-the-clock curfew imposed on more than a million Palestinians, during which the IDF killed a further 76 Palestinians, mostly stone-throwing youths (*Washington Report on Middle East Affairs*, June 1994). The Israeli journalist Danny Rubenstein was later to argue that the Hebron killings 'directly and immediately created the chain of suicide bombings and the appalling upward spiral composed of Israeli responses and Palestinian counter-responses' (*Ha'aretz*, 28 September 1998). In the wake of these events the Israeli government, under pressure from the Palestinians and sections of Israeli public opinion, moved to outlaw the overtly racist Kach party, but refused Palestinian demands to remove the few hundred heavily armed and guarded settlers who lived among more than 100,000 Palestinians in Hebron. The Israeli government also refused PLO requests to put the issue of settlements on the negotiating table, arguing that under the Declaration of Principles it was not obliged to do so until the third year of the interim period. Hamas vowed revenge for the Hebron killings, and shortly before the signing of the next stage of the interim agreements in Cairo in May 1994 it carried out a car bombing in Afula, which killed eight and the first-ever suicide bombing in Israel, which killed five people. Suicide bombings involved individuals strapping explosives, nails and ball bearings to their bodies, which were then detonated in densely packed areas such as markets or buses. This new and indiscriminate weapon left those who survived permanently scarred or disabled and significantly intensified security fears among Israelis. A report from a *BBC1* News bulletin describes the aftermath of a suicide attack on a crowded Israeli market:

The two explosions came within seconds of each other, cutting down scores of people in the heart of the crowded market. It was just after one o'clock and the market was full of shoppers. Streams of ambulances came to carry away the dead and the injured. It was a place of appalling suffering ... Those who escaped injury were led away from the devastation and others arrived desperate to see if their friends and relatives had escaped the carnage. (BBC1, Evening News, 30 July 1997)

Some Palestinians have tried to justify such attacks by arguing that they are in response to the killing of Palestinian civilians by Israelis. Others have argued that they are resisting an illegal occupation, or that it is the only effective weapon against a much more powerful adversary. Dr Eyad El-Sarraj, a psychiatrist and winner of the 1998 Martin Ennals human rights award, has noted that most suicide bombers had suffered a severe trauma when young, 'often the torture of a close relative' and that 'children grow up wanting to take revenge for their trauma. Torture is an integral part of that cycle of violence' (*Guardian*, 24 January 2003). Whatever the motivations or factors behind suicide bombings, human rights groups have unequivocally condemned such attacks and demanded that those involved in planning attacks be brought to justice. In a report entitled *Without Distinction: Attacks on civilians by Palestinian armed groups*, Amnesty International argues that indiscriminate attacks on civilians cannot be justified whatever the circumstances or provocation:

The obligation to protect civilians is absolute and cannot be set aside because Israel has failed to respect its obligations. The attacks against civilians by Palestinian armed groups are widespread, systematic and in pursuit of an explicit policy to attack civilians. They therefore constitute crimes against humanity under international law. They may also constitute war crimes, depending on the legal characterisation of the hostilities and interpretation of the status of Palestinian armed groups and fighters under international humanitarian law. (Amnesty International, 2002a)

THE CAIRO AGREEMENT, OSLO II AND THE ISRAEL–JORDAN PEACE TREATY

The agreement signed in Cairo on 4 May 1994 concluded the Gaza and Jericho phase of the redeployment and set the terms for expanding Palestinian autonomy in the West Bank. This had three stages. Firstly, the Palestinian National Authority was to take charge of a number of municipal functions; secondly, the IDF would withdraw from population centres, and, finally, there would be Palestinian elections for a new authority. However, Palestinian negotiators were disappointed with the new agreement. They had hoped that Israel would replace the complex system of military ordinances and occupation laws with the Fourth Geneva Convention and international law within the occupied territories, but this was not forthcoming (Shlaim, 2000). The United Nations Commission on Human Rights continued to be critical of Israeli human rights abuses in the territories. In 1994, it issued a resolution 'condemning' settler and IDF killings, torture, imprisonment without trial, house demolitions and land expropriations, curfews, collective punishments and restrictions on movement and settlement-building (United Nations, 1994).

The construction of illegal Jewish settlements had accelerated following the election of the Rabin administration in 1992. Between 1992 and 1995 the settler population in the occupied territories (excluding East Jerusalem) rose from 74,800 to 136,000 (*Foundation for Middle East Peace*, 1997). Palestinians believed that increased settlement-building and expropriations of Palestinian land was a violation of the spirit if not the letter of the Oslo Accords, and would ultimately prejudice the possibility of a viable Palestinian state. The American historian and Middle East commentator Geoffrey Aronson argued that 'there is no missing the fact that Rabin's settlement drive is aimed at putting the future of the city [Jerusalem] and its West Bank environs beyond the reach of diplomacy' (*Report on Israeli Settlement in the Occupied Territory*, May 1995). He also cited statements from the Israeli commentator Ze'ev Schiff that 'when we come to the final stage [of negotiations] nothing will be left [in Jerusalem] for the Palestinians to negotiate, apart from the Islamic holy places'. Rabin's administration also embarked on a process of building bypass roads linking settlements, which could only be used by Jewish settlers and the IDF. This plan, Israel Shahak (1995) claimed, was originally conceived by Ariel Sharon in 1977 but was finally implemented by Rabin directly after the Declaration of Principles. He argued that its purpose was to create a matrix of control whereby all the Arab population centres were split into enclaves criss-crossed by the roads and settlement blocks so that the Israeli army would be able to control the discontinuous cantons 'from outside'. Tel-Aviv University professor Tanya Reinhart argued that Rabin's policies 'resemble[d] the beginning of Apartheid rather than its end' and were 'almost identical' to the South African Bantustan model (*Ha'aretz*, 27 May 1994). The construction of the bypass road network also allowed the Israeli government to enforce closures on the Palestinian areas, which restricted Palestinian movement and access to employment. Israel justified such measures by arguing that it was necessary to prevent attacks by Palestinians against Israelis. It did, however, have very serious effects on the Palestinian economy. The Israeli journalist Nadav Ha'etzni reported that by May 1995 curfews and closures had 'devastated the Palestinian economy and destroyed 100,000 families in Gaza alone' (*Ma'ariv*, 5 May 1995, cited in Chomsky, 1999: 548). The deteriorating economic situation for Palestinians was compounded by Israeli moves to achieve 'separation' by replacing Palestinian workers with migrant labour from Thailand, the Philippines, Romania and other parts of Eastern Europe. Such factors, Shlaim suggests, 'actually worsened the situation in the occupied territories and confounded Palestinian aspirations for a state of their own' (2000: 530). Furthermore there was no halt to the bloodshed on both sides. Between the signing of the Declaration of Principles in September 1993 and the end of 1994, 93 Israelis and 194 Palestinians were killed in violent incidents (B'Tselem, 2003a).

In September 1994, Israel and Jordan concluded a peace treaty that normalised relations between the two countries. The agreement set the international border between Israel and Jordan and settled water disputes relating to the Yarmouk and Jordan Rivers. The treaty marked the second comprehensive treaty that Israel had signed with its Arab neighbours.

In late September 1995, Yasser Arafat and Yitzak Rabin concluded the next stage of the interim agreement under which the West Bank was divided into three areas. Area A

(3 per cent of the West Bank, incorporating Nablus, Jenin, Tulkarem, Qalqilya, Ramallah, Bethlehem and subsequently, in January 1997, 80 per cent of Hebron) would have its civilian administration and internal security controlled by the Palestinian Authority. Area B (23 per cent of the West Bank, comprising 440 villages and surrounding lands) was to have certain municipal functions administered by the Palestinian Authority while security would be dealt with by joint Palestinian–Israeli patrols. Area C (74 per cent of the West Bank, including all of the 145 Jewish settlements including those in and around East Jerusalem) would remain under complete Israeli control.

On 4 November 1995, Yitzak Rabin was assassinated by a 25-year-old settler, Yigal Amir. After the killing the unrepentant Amir accused Rabin of selling out the settlers and preparing to give away the occupied territories to the Palestinians. Rabin was succeeded as prime minister by Shimon Peres who pledged to maintain the momentum of the peace process. No Israelis had been killed in suicide attacks since the 21 August bombing in Jerusalem that had killed three Israelis and an American. Mishal and Sela (2000) suggest that both Hamas and Islamic Jihad were under pressure from both the Palestinian Authority and Israel, and did not want to antagonise Palestinian public opinion by precipitating a halt to the scheduled Israeli redeployments. Mishal and Sela also note that militant groups had been pushing for 'a conditional cease-fire with Israel to stop the bloodshed of innocents on both sides' (2000: 71). In early 1996 Peres ordered the killing of Yahya Ayyash, a Hamas leader who had previously masterminded several suicide attacks, which had killed approximately 60 Israelis. Shlaim claims that the Israeli media had exaggerated his status, presenting him as 'public enemy number one' while 'omitting to mention that the attacks he organized came as a response to the [Hebron] massacre' (2000: 556). The assassination of Ayyash using a booby-trapped phone led to Hamas vowing revenge, and there followed six suicide bombings in February and March 1996, which left 62 Israelis dead (Israeli Ministry of Foreign Affairs, 1999). Peres's popularity declined under attacks from the right, and he moved to suspend talks with the newly elected Palestinian Authority and closed the borders to all workers from the occupied territories.

Shortly afterwards Peres launched a major offensive against Hezbullah in Southern Lebanon where Israel had been fighting a long guerrilla war. Hezbullah claimed it was fighting to end the illegal Israeli occupation of Southern Lebanon, which had been ongoing since 1978, in violation of UN Security Council Resolution 425.[43] Israel claimed that Hezbullah was intent on the destruction of the Israeli state. Casualty statistics suggest that Palestinian and Lebanese civilians had suffered disproportionately in the conflict. In the period between 1985 and 1996 the Israeli army estimates that Hezbullah guerrilla and rocket attacks had killed six Israeli civilians (Israeli Defence Force, 2003). In a single operation in 1993 Amnesty International (1996a) reported that Israel killed 118 Lebanese civilians and that 300,000 people were displaced. The journalist and former chief inspector of the US Information Agency, Richard Curtiss, suggests that after this operation, unwritten rules of engagement were crafted by the US State Department's Warren Christopher, with both sides agreeing to confine attacks to combatants in South Lebanon (*Washington Report on Middle East Affairs*, May/June 1996).

On 11 April 1996, Peres launched Operation 'Grapes of Wrath'. This was claimed to be in retaliation for rocket strikes on Israeli settlements that had injured 34 civilians and other attacks, which had killed eight members of the IDF in Southern Lebanon. Hezbullah's view was that it had a right to resist the Israeli troops illegally occupying Southern Lebanon, and that the rockets fired on Israeli towns and villages were in retaliation for the killing by Israel of three Lebanese civilians. The Israeli operation involved more than a thousand air sorties and 16,000 shells against fewer than 500 Hezbullah fighters (*Ha'aretz*, 21 May 1996). Curtiss claims that many of the attacks were 'targeted at electric power plants and relay stations, bridges, and other parts of Lebanon's war-battered basic infrastructure' (*Washington Report on Middle East Affairs*, May/June 1996). The Israeli journalist Avi Shavit alleges that 400,000 civilians were forced to flee their homes in eight hours, after which the Israeli air force treated the abandoned properties as military targets and shelled them (*Ha'aretz*, 21 May 1996).

On 18 April, Israel bombed the UN compound at Qana, killing 106 refugees who had sought sanctuary there. Israel stated that the bombing, which involved anti-personnel munitions, was a mistake and that the real target was an area nearby, where Hezbullah fighters had been operating. Reports both from the UN (1996) and Amnesty International (1996b) found that the attack on the UN compound was unlikely to have been accidental and also condemned Israeli missile attacks on ambulances and residential areas, which killed many civilians. Shlaim suggests that the operation was an attempt by Shimon Peres to revive his flagging political fortunes and recast himself 'as the hard man of Israeli politics ahead of the crucial general elections' (2000: 560). However, it did nothing to revive his political fortunes and the following month he was beaten in the general election by the Likud candidate Binyamin Netanyahu.

THE NETANYAHU ADMINISTRATION

Netanyahu's attitude towards the peace process before his election had been one of undisguised antipathy. He had campaigned publicly against its implementation in speeches and in print, and had been accused by Rabin's widow of inciting his assassination by making inflammatory public speeches, which likened Rabin to an SS officer. His coalition included the far-right and settler groups who called for the forced deportation of all Palestinians from the occupied territories. Netanyahu's central argument was that the peace process had illustrated Israel's weakness, reduced the deterrent power of the IDF and damaged the nation's security. He argued that Israel had adhered to the Oslo formula while the Palestinians had failed to keep their side of the bargain, by failing to dismantle militant organisations, collect their weapons or extradite their members to Israel. Netanyahu's alternative was to renegotiate the redeployments that had been agreed in principle. He argued that these threatened Israel's security and that 'whatever the officials of the previous Labor administration had whispered in Palestinian ears was irrelevant' (Netanyahu, 2000: 343). He was also against full statehood for the Palestinians, arguing that Israel had to control the exit and entry points to the Palestinian entity as well as its airspace, plus much of the Jordan Valley and the West Bank water supply. He also suggested that Arab nations should resettle the Palestinian refugees. Shlaim claims that as soon as he took power Netanyahu began to renege on Israel's Oslo obligations:

> Serious deterioration occurred in Israel's relations with the Palestinians as a result of Netanyahu's backtracking. He adopted a 'work-to-rule' approach designed to undermine the Oslo process. There was no Israeli pullout from Hebron, no 'opening of the safe passage' route from Gaza to the West Bank, and no discussion of the further West Bank redeployment that Israel had pledged to carry out in early September. Instead Palestinian homes without an Israeli permit were demolished in east Jerusalem, and plans were approved for the construction of new Israeli settlements. The quality of life for the Palestinians deteriorated progressively, and hopes for a better future were all but extinguished. (2000: 576)

In October 1996, violence erupted in Jerusalem when Netanyahu ordered the blasting open of an archaeological tunnel close to the Al-Aqsa Mosque. This was taken by Palestinians as a statement of sovereignty over Islamic holy sites and triggered disturbances in which 15 Israeli soldiers and 80 Palestinians were killed, and a further 1,500 Palestinians wounded. Under pressure from the Americans Netanyahu agreed to the delayed redeployment of Israeli troops from Hebron in January 1997 by signing the Hebron protocol, which also committed Israel to three further redeployments in the West Bank over the next 18 months. Under the agreement Hebron was split into Jewish and Arab zones. The Jewish zone reserved for the 450 settlers constituted 20 per cent of the city, including its best commercial areas. The remaining 80 per cent of the city was reserved for the 130,000 Palestinian residents of Hebron who were subject to frequent curfews and restrictions on movement.

After the signing of the Hebron protocol Netanyahu approved a number of new settlements. In February 1997, he announced plans for 6,500 new dwellings for 30,000 settlers at Jabal Ghneim (Har Homa) on the outskirts of annexed East Jerusalem. Har Homa would complete the chain of concentric settlements around Jerusalem and cut off Arab East Jerusalem from the rest of the West Bank. The move was met with anger from Palestinians and condemned by the UN (1997) General Assembly by 130 votes to two (Israel, United States). Palestinians were unhappy with more expropriation of their land and called a general strike in protest. The US twice vetoed Security Council resolutions condemning the project, while the General Assembly passed further resolutions calling for a halt to the Har Homa project, the removal of settlements in the occupied territories, and the application of the Fourth Geneva Convention within the territories. None of these moves stopped the construction of the new settlements. In June 1997 the Israeli journalist Jay Bushinsky reported that Netanyahu had outlined his 'Allon Plus' plan for a possible settlement with the Palestinians. The plan involved Israel annexing approximately 60 per cent of the West Bank which would include Greater Jerusalem, the hills east of Jerusalem, the Jordan Valley, the settlements and all the bypass roads connecting them, plus permanent Israeli control of the West Bank water supply (*Jerusalem Post*, 5 June 1997). The proposals were met with dismay by Palestinian leaders who accused Israel of violating the Oslo Accords and trying to destroy the peace process.

Although the conflict between Palestinian fighters and the IDF and settlers in the occupied territories continued to claim more lives, there were no suicide attacks in Israel between March 1996 and March 1997. Between 21 March 1997 and 4 September 1997 militants carried out three suicide attacks, killing 24 Israelis. Hamas representatives argued that the attacks were the only way to stop the expropriation of more Palestinian land for settlement-building and the 'Judaisation' of the holy places. On 23 September 1997 the Hamas leadership sent a letter to Netanyahu, delivered by King Hussein of Jordan, in which Hamas suggested setting up an indirect dialogue with the Israeli government that would be mediated by King Hussein. The purpose of the dialogue would be to achieve a cessation of violence as well as a 'discussion of all matters' (*Ha'aretz,* 9 October 1997, cited in Mishal & Sela, 2000: 72). Two days later Netanyahu ordered the killing of the head of Hamas's Political Bureau, Khalid Mash'al, in Jordan. The attempted assassination by two Mossad agents was botched and Mash'al's bodyguard captured the two assassins who were later traded for the imprisoned Hamas spiritual leader Sheikh Ahmed Yassin. The attempted killing soured relations with King Hussein, Israel's closest ally in the Arab world, and ended this opportunity for a ceasefire. The release of Yassin followed by his return to Gaza strengthened Hamas's support.

In March 1998, 1,500 Israeli reservists including twelve retired major-generals called on Netanyahu to stop settlement-building and try to end the conflict and normalise relations (Shlaim, 2000). However, Netanyahu cancelled the scheduled Israeli redeployments, citing security concerns. Despite efforts by both Britain and the US to revive the process it ground to a halt. Both sides in the conflict accused the other of bad faith in reneging on their Oslo obligations. Netanyahu reiterated his claims that the PLO had failed to disarm or arrest militant groups, prevent attacks against Israelis and amend the PLO charter. Others contested this. Tanya Reinhart, writing in the Jewish magazine *Tikkun*, claimed that Arafat had taken strong action against Hamas and that this was recognised by Israel's security services:

> Arafat's security services carried out this job [maintaining Israeli security] faithfully, by assassinating Hamas terrorists (disguised as 'accidents'), and arresting Hamas political leaders ... Ample information was published in the Israeli media regarding these activities, and 'security sources' were full of praises for Arafat's achievements. For example, Ami Ayalon, then head of the Israeli secret service (Shabak), announced, in a government meeting on April 5, 1998 that 'Arafat is doing his job – he is fighting terror and puts all his weight against the Hamas' (*Ha'aretz*, 6 April 1998). The rate of success of the Israeli security services in containing terror was never higher than that of Arafat; in fact, it was probably much lower. (March/April 2002)

In a 1998 report, the Israeli peace group Gush Shalom (1998) blamed the Netanyahu administration for the breakdown in the peace process and accused the government of 19 separate violations of the Oslo Accords. These included settlement and bypass road building, use of closures, failure to release Palestinian prisoners, torture and other human rights abuses, and failure to undertake scheduled military withdrawals or move towards final-status negotiations. During this period support for organisations such as Islamic Jihad and Hamas grew while the PLO and particularly Yasser Arafat lost popularity. Partly this was because of corruption scandals that engulfed the PLO leadership, which was accused of nepotism and siphoning off funds meant for the Palestinian Authority. It was also because of Arafat's autocratic style and the serious human rights abuses committed by the Palestinian security forces who were using torture and engaging in extra-judicial killings against suspected militants. There was also widespread anger that Arafat had failed to stop settlement-building. Geoffrey Aronson claimed that Arafat and the other PLO 'outsiders' (those from outside the occupied territories) failed to appreciate the significance of the settlements:

> PA chairman Yasser Arafat is briefed infrequently on Israel's settlement policy, and his response is generally stunned silence as he looks at the maps depicting the dimensions of the enterprise. Palestinian Authority negotiators Mahmoud Abbas (Abu Mazen) and Ahmad Quray (Abu Ala) have never been on a 'settlement tour.' If one is to judge by their negotiating priorities, they have no concept of the role of settlements in the history of Israel's policies in the occupied territories, nor do they believe that such an understanding is required. (*Report on Israeli Settlement in the Occupied Territories*, July/August 1998)

In October 1998, Israel and Palestinian negotiators concluded the next phase of the peace process, signing the Wye Accords in Maryland. Israel undertook to redeploy its troops from a further 13 per cent of the West Bank in three stages. The Palestinians agreed to amend the parts of the Palestinian National Charter calling for Israel's destruction and to work with Israeli security services and the CIA to improve Israel's security. The security component of the agreement was heavily criticised by human rights groups both before and after the signing, who argued it was likely to increase human rights abuses such as torture and imprisonment without trial.[44] The Wye Accords passed in the Knesset by a large majority, though Netanyahu received virtually no support for the agreement among his right-wing/religious coalition. Although both parties to the agreement had agreed not to undertake 'unilateral actions' to change the status of the occupied territories, members of Netanyahu's coalition publicly called on settler groups to take as much land as possible to keep it out of Palestinian hands. Ariel Sharon, the infrastructure minister, told a Tsomet party gathering on 15 November that 'Everyone should take action, should run, should grab more hills ... We'll expand the area. Whatever is seized will be ours. Whatever isn't seized will end up in their hands' (*BBC News Online*, 16 November 1998). Netanyahu promoted the same policies, though less overtly: 'There is no such thing as a freeze [on construction] .... Our policy is to grow and expand ... This issue must be coordinated behind closed doors with the army and not in front of the media' (*Ha'aretz*, 24 November 1998). On 20 December 1998, the Israeli government suspended the second redeployment stipulated in the Wye Accords unless the Palestinian Authority met five conditions, most of which were new. Netanyahu claimed that it was necessary to suspend the redeployments to safeguard Israel's security. Shlaim suggests the move was intended to 'torpedo the peace process and put the blame on the Palestinians' (2000: 605). Three days later the Knesset voted to dissolve itself and schedule new elections for May 1999.

THE BARAK ADMINISTRATION

The May elections brought Labor's Ehud Barak to power. Three months into Barak's tenure the American journalist Deborah Sontag reported that his administration had 'authorized new construction in the West Bank's Jewish settlements at a pace

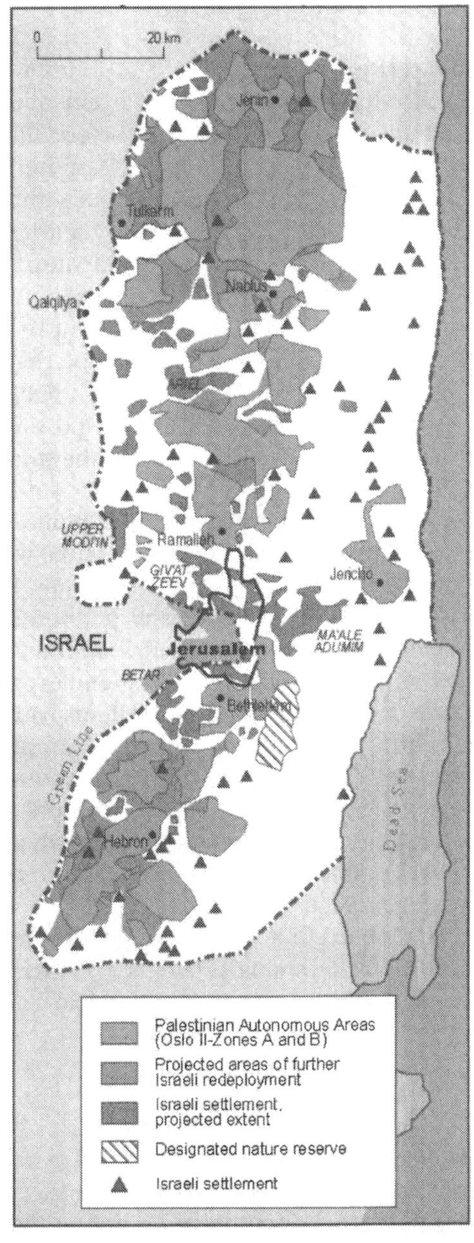

Map 5 Wye Memorandum, 1998 (Wye Accords map)

exceeding that of the right-wing administration of Benjamin Netanyahu' (*New York Times*, 28 September 1999). Barak also moved to initiate negotiations with Syria rather than with the Palestinians, which the Palestinians took as a snub and an attempt to pressurise them. Barak argued that he pursued the Syrian track first because this problem was considered less intractable and, secondly, because Syria with its large army and non-conventional weapons was considered an 'existential threat' (*New York Review of Books*, 9 August 2001). After four months of negotiations the peace talks between Israel and Syria collapsed without a settlement. Both parties blamed the other.[45] In May 2000, Barak took the decision to withdraw the Israeli army and its proxy forces from South Lebanon. The occupying Israeli army had been taking increasingly heavy casualties from Hezbullah guerrilla raids and the losses were politically unpopular. Rachelle Marshall suggests that the withdrawal allowed hundreds of thousands of Lebanese refugees to return to their devastated villages, and Hezbullah to set up medical facilities and begin rebuilding the civilian infrastructure (*Washington Report on Middle East Affairs*, July 2000).

Following the failure of the Syrian track, Barak turned his attention to the Palestinians. Barak's tenure (up until the outbreak of the second intifada) had seen a decline in attacks by Palestinian militants and no suicide attacks (B'Tselem, 2003a). In early 2000, Marshall claims that Barak suspended a number of Israel's Oslo commitments. These included the scheduled release of 1,650 Palestinian prisoners arrested before the Oslo process began and the scheduled handover to Palestinian control of three small villages bordering Jerusalem, Abu Dis, Al Ezzariyye and Swarah (*Washington Report on Middle East Affairs*, July 2000). Instead, she notes that Barak authorised the seizure of 162 acres from these villages for the construction of a new bypass road linking settlement blocks to Jerusalem and the construction of 200 Jewish housing units in Abu Dis. Barak also decided to renegotiate the agreements that the PLO had signed with Netanyahu and cancelled the third partial redeployment of Israeli troops. The Oslo Accords had specified that by the time that final-status talks began, Israel should have withdrawn from approximately 90 per cent of the occupied territories, but by the end of May 2000 the figure was only 18 per cent.

In March 2000, as preparatory talks between Israeli and Palestinian delegations on final-status issues were beginning, 120 Palestinian intellectuals and cultural figures sent an open letter to the 'Israeli and Jewish Public' calling for a just solution to be based on either the 1967 borders or a bi-national state. It argued that 'one side believes the present balance of power to be in its favour and that it can impose a humiliating agreement on the other side, forcing it to accept virtually anything it chooses to enforce' (*Ha'aretz*, 13 March 2000). The Israeli commentator Danny Rabinowitz argued that the letter revealed the deep chasm between Israeli and Palestinian evaluations of the peace process:

> One view, which is accepted by the majority of Israelis, considers Oslo a positive, symmetric process: an elected government in Israel is conducting peace negotiations with a Palestinian leadership that reflects the true interests of the Palestinian people. Pursuing this joint path will ultimately lead to a durable peace between the two peoples. The second view, which is asserted by the signatories to the letter, considers Oslo an inherently asymmetric process whose forgone conclusion is not only unfair, but also dangerous. The gist here is that Israel, which is strong, big, rich and backed by a superpower, is conducting negotiations of a coercive nature with a weak Palestinian leadership that has sold out. Arafat, his aides and the few thousand families that are close to his government are mere puppets with no will of their own and without the ability to engage in true diplomatic manoeuvring. The corruption and despotism constantly being exposed in the economy, judicial system, human rights record and other areas of the Palestinian Authority demonstrate that the thrust of the leadership in the West Bank and Gaza is to preserve its own rule and to divvy up the financial and symbolic spoils flowing in from donor nations. This view of the process sees the true national interest of millions of Palestinians in the territories and the Diaspora ground into the dust. (*Ha'aretz*, 19 March 2000)

In the run-up to the final-status talks in May 2000, Israel released maps of a projected final settlement indicating that Palestinian self-rule would be limited to three or four discontinuous pieces of territory.

THE CAMP DAVID FINAL-STATUS TALKS

On 11 July 2000 Yasser Arafat and Ehud Barak met for final-status negotiations at Camp David in the USA. After two weeks the talks broke down amid bitter recriminations. Israel argued that it had made a 'generous offer' to return 97 per cent of the occupied territories, which the other party spurned, turning to violence to force concessions it could not achieve at the negotiating table. The Palestinians argued that the offer was vague and unacceptable, 'less than a Bantustan', in Arafat's words (*New York Times*, 26 July 2001). Analysing the conference is difficult because all of Israel's offers were made orally, with no maps or written proposals presented.

In an interview with Israeli historian Benny Morris, Ehud Barak laid out the Israeli perspective on the failure of the talks (*New York Review of Books*, 9 August 2001). Barak claimed that he had offered Arafat 92 per cent of the West Bank and 100 per cent of the Gaza Strip, together with some territorial compensation from pre-1967 Israel. He denied that the state would consist of Bantustans. Instead he argued that although the West Bank would be sliced in two by a 'razor thin Israeli wedge' running from the settlement of Maale Adumin to the Jordan River, 'Palestinian territorial continuity would have been assured by a tunnel or bridge'. He also claimed to have offered to dismantle most of the settlements and concentrate the bulk of the settlers in the 8 per cent of the West Bank that was to be annexed to Israel. A Palestinian capital would be set up in East Jerusalem, with some neighbourhoods to become Palestinian territory and others to enjoy 'functional autonomy'. The Palestinians, it is claimed, were offered custodianship though not sovereignty over the Temple Mount. Barak also alleged that Israel offered a right of return for Palestinian refugees to the prospective Palestinian state, though no admission of Israeli responsibility for the creation of the refugee problem and no return of any refugees to Israel. Barak accused Arafat of saying no to every

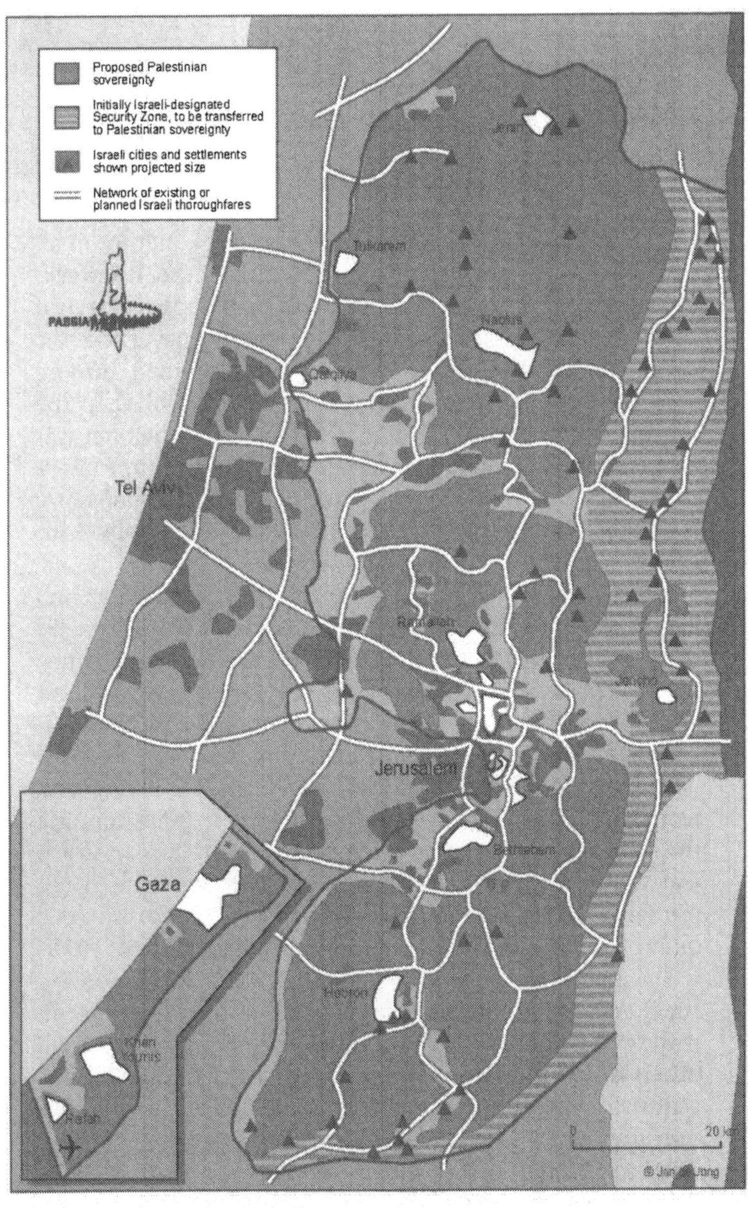

Map 6 Projection of the West Bank Final-Status Map, presented by Israel, Camp David, July 2000

proposal and offering no counterproposals. Barak also claimed that Arafat believed that Israel 'has no right to exist and he seeks its demise'. This, argued Barak, would be achieved by using the Palestinian refugees as a demographic tool to subvert the Israeli state. He also accused Arabs in general, and Arafat in particular, of being 'a product of a culture in which to tell a lie ... creates no dissonance', because Arabs 'don't suffer from the problem of telling lies that exists in Judeo-Christian culture'. In Arab societies, he stated, 'there is no such thing as "the truth".' In making this charge, Barak had perhaps overlooked the comments of Yitzak Shamir, when responding to a charge of dishonesty. He was quoted in *Ha'aretz* as saying that 'for the sake of the land of Israel, it is permissible to lie' (14 February 1992, cited in Shlaim, 2000: 496). Barak also suggested that it would probably take eighty years from 1948 before the Palestinians were ready to make the necessary compromises for peace, because of what Barak described as a 'salmon syndrome' among Palestinians. Eighty years after 1948 the Palestinians who experienced displacement at first hand will have largely died, so there will be 'very few "salmons" around who will still want to return to their birthplaces to die'.

Robert Malley, a special adviser to President Clinton, and Hussein Agha, the Oxford historian, have criticised Barak's analysis as 'remarkably shallow' (*New York Review of Books*, 9 August 2001). They suggest that all the protagonists share some responsibility for the failure of the talks. Malley and Agha argue that Barak's decision to renege on Israel's interim commitments, such as troop withdrawals and prisoner releases while expanding settlements, was designed to reduce political friction from the Israeli right in the lead up to the talks and to husband political capital. He could then present 'all concessions and all rewards in one comprehensive package that the Israeli public would be asked to accept in a national referendum'. This 'all or nothing' approach, Malley and Agha allege, put Arafat under tremendous pressure from powerful Palestinian constituencies such as the security establishment, intellectuals, civil servants and the business community who had lost faith in Barak. They also suggest that Barak's refusal to withdraw from territory scheduled in the interim agreements directly affected the perceived balance of power, because the Palestinians believed that they would also have to negotiate over that land in the final-status talks. Malley and Agha maintain that all of these factors left Arafat with the impression that the Israelis and Americans were trying to 'dupe' him into accepting a humiliating deal and led him to adopt a siege mentality, unamenable to fluid negotiations and the presentation of counterproposals. They also suggest that not enough time had gone into laying the groundwork with preparatory negotiations prior to the summit and that a month prior to the talks Arafat had warned US Secretary of State Madeleine Albright that because of all these factors the talks were very likely to fail.

Other commentators, such as the Israeli human rights group Gush Shalom (2003), have questioned whether a 'generous deal' was offered to Palestinians. They argue that Palestinians made their historic compromise at Oslo in agreeing to cede to Israel 78 per cent of mandatory Palestine, and that they were never offered 95 per cent of the occupied territories at Camp David in July 2000. Gush Shalom alleges that Barak insisted on annexing 10 per cent of the West Bank comprised of settlement blocks, which it noted would 'create impossible borders which severely disrupt Palestinian life in the West Bank'. It also suggests that Barak wanted 'temporary Israeli control' of another 10 per cent of the West Bank for an unspecified duration. Gush Shalom argues that 'what appears to be territorial continuity is actually split up by settlement blocs, bypass roads and roadblocks' and that 'the Palestinians have to relinquish land reserves essential for their development and absorption of refugees' as well as accepting 'Israeli supervision of border crossings together with many other restrictions'. It suggests that nobody would accept foreign control of domestic border crossings or travelling 50 miles between areas when the real distance was only five miles.

Jeff Halper, an anthropology professor at Ben-Gurion University, and coordinator of the Israeli Committee against House Demolitions, argues that the focus on whether the

Palestinians were offered 81 per cent or 91 per cent or 95 per cent or 96 per cent is misplaced, because even if Israel agreed to hand back 96 per cent of the occupied territories it would still possess a 'matrix of control', which would completely undermine Palestinian sovereignty and independent development:

What is the matrix of control? It is an interlocking series of mechanisms, only a few of which require physical occupation of territory, that allow Israel to control every aspect of Palestinian life in the Occupied Territories. The matrix works like the Japanese game of Go. Instead of defeating your opponent as in chess, in Go you win by immobilizing your opponent, by gaining control of key points of a matrix so that every time s/he moves s/he encounters an obstacle of some kind ... The matrix imposed by Israel in the West Bank, Gaza and East Jerusalem, similar in appearance to a Go board, has virtually paralysed the Palestinian population without 'defeating' it or even conquering much territory. (*Middle East Report*, Fall 2000)

Part of this matrix, argues Halper, involves the expansion of 'Metropolitan' Jerusalem, which, he suggests, stretches almost all the way to the Jordan River and incorporates 40 per cent of the West Bank, including Ramallah and Bethlehem. Halper suggests that Israeli control of this area, which cuts off Palestinians in East Jerusalem from the rest of the West Bank, 'renders the sovereignty of a future Palestinian state meaningless'. Halper also points to the grid of bypass roads criss-crossing the West Bank linking settlements, which would also require a substantial permanent Israeli military presence across the Palestinian state. All of these factors, suggested Halper, meant that even if Yasser Arafat had agreed to Barak's proposals at Camp David, the agreement would not have held:

The issue in the Israeli–Palestinian negotiations, then, is not simply territory – it revolves around questions of control, viability and justice. A Palestinian state carved into small, disconnected enclaves, surrounded and indeed truncated by massive Israeli settlement blocs, subject to Israeli military and economic closures, unable to offer justice to its dispersed people and without its most sacred symbols of religion and identity, can hardly be called a viable state. 'Peace' may be imposed, but unless it is just it will not be lasting.

The breakdown of the Camp David talks was followed by months of secret negotiations between Palestinian and Israeli officials. Then, on 28 September 2000, another decisive event was precipitated by a key figure on the Israeli right. Ariel Sharon and other members of the Likud leadership together with 1,000 armed police visited Islam's third holiest site, the Al-Haram al-Sharif. Palestinians considered this visit to be a statement of sovereignty over one of the Muslim world's holiest sites and a provocative gesture from an Israeli leader notorious for his role in the Sabra and Shatila massacres. It was followed by riots and fighting, from which developed the second intifada.

SEPTEMBER 2000: THE SECOND INTIFADA

The factors behind this outbreak are as usual contested. The conservative commentator Charles Krauthammer suggested that Yasser Arafat himself planned and orchestrated the intifada in order to win concessions he could not secure at the Camp David negotiating table:

> The plain fact is that Yasser Arafat, thrown on the diplomatic defensive by rejecting Barak's offer (to the astonishment and dismay of the American mediators), has done what he has always done: resort to violence to regain the initiative and, most important, mint new underage martyrs – on world television – to regain the international sympathy he had forfeited by turning down peace at Camp David ... The war that followed was as spontaneous as a Havana demonstration. The preacher at the al-Aqsa mosque called at Friday prayers to 'eradicate the Jews from Palestine'. Official Palestinian television began playing over and over archival footage of the Palestinian intifada of 1987–1993 showing young people out in the streets throwing stones. In case one still didn't get the message, Voice of Palestine radio began playing patriotic war songs. Arafat then closed the schools and declared a general strike, causing everyone to go out into the street. With Arafat's chief political lieutenant on the West Bank orchestrating the militias, war then 'broke out'. (*Jewish World Review*, 6 October 2000)

Others suggested that the intifada was a spontaneous people's uprising triggered by Sharon's visit and inflamed by Israel's decision to use live ammunition against predominately unarmed demonstrators. The situation was especially serious as Arafat's police ended up firing at the Israeli security forces. The Israeli journalist Amira Hass argues the intifada represented the explosion of seven years of Palestinian frustration at the failures of the Oslo process to end the military occupation, and that Arafat was powerless to stand in its way:

> Seven years after the Oslo accord, all Palestinians feel betrayed, because they are still living under occupation ... When six Palestinians were killed by close-range bullets at the mosque by Israeli police, the anger which swept everybody contained all other angers, of seven years and longer. This time Arafat could not dream of checking the spreading anger with his security forces. After all, it was about Al Aqsa. All his credibility would have been lost, so he ordered the policemen to stop. Even without an order, his policemen were unable to restrain their fire, while watching Palestinian youngsters being shot in their eyes and heads by the hundreds. Even if the clashes are subdued, the Palestinians now demand a change in the rules of the game. And their message is meant not only for Israel but for Arafat too. (*Guardian*, 3 October 2005)

The Israeli academic and journalist Tanya Reinhart suggests that the intifada was deliberately provoked by prominent Israeli military leaders because they wanted to launch a war against the Palestinians in order to destroy the Palestinian Authority and topple Arafat (*Tikkun*, March 2002). Their ultimate aim, according to Reinhart, was to prevent the emergence of a Palestinian state and retain the occupied territories. She suggests that the subsequent invasion by Israel of Ramallah, Jenin and other West Bank cities in 2003 and the almost complete destruction of the infrastructure of the nascent Palestinian National Authority during these attacks appear to correlate very closely with the 'Field of Thorns' plan, which had been circulating among Israeli military and political leaders from 1996 onwards:

Already in October 2000, at the outset of the Palestinian uprising, military circles were ready with detailed operative plans to topple Arafat and the Palestinian Authority. This was before the Palestinian terror attacks started. A document prepared by the security services, at the request of then PM Barak, stated on October 15, 2000 that 'Arafat, the person, is a severe threat to the security of the state [of Israel] and the damage which will result from his disappearance is less than the damage caused by his existence.' (Details of the document were published in *Ma'ariv*, July 6, 2001.) The operative plan, known as 'Fields of Thorns' had been prepared back in 1996, and was then updated during the Intifada. (Amir Oren, *Ha'aretz*, Nov. 23, 2001.) The political echelon for its part (Barak's circles), worked on preparing public opinion to the toppling of Arafat ... *The Foreign Report* (Jane's Defense Information publication) of July 12, 2001 disclosed that the Israeli army (under Sharon's government) has updated its plans for an 'all-out assault to smash the Palestinian authority, force out leader Yasser Arafat and kill or detain its army.' The blueprint, titled 'The Destruction of the Palestinian Authority and Disarmament of All Armed Forces,' was presented to the Israeli government by chief of staff Shaul Mofaz, on July 8 [2001]. The assault would be launched, at the government's discretion, after a big suicide bomb attack in Israel, causing widespread deaths and injuries, citing the bloodshed as justification. (*Tikkun*, March 2002)

On 7 October 2000, the UN Security Council passed Resolution 1322 condemning both Ariel Sharon's visit to the Al-Haram al-Sharif, and Israel's 'excessive use of force against Palestinians'. There was also criticism of the Israeli response to Palestinian demonstrations from human rights groups such as Amnesty International, Human Rights Watch and B'Tselem. An investigation by Amnesty International had found that the 'majority of [Palestinian] people killed were taking part in demonstrations where stones were the only weapon used'. Amnesty also reported that groups of civilians including children appeared, 'on many occasions, to have been deliberately targeted' (Amnesty, 2000b). Accusations that Israeli soldiers deliberately shot and killed unarmed civilians including children were also made by Israeli soldiers themselves, some of whom refused to serve in the occupied territories because they did not want to take part in such alleged activities.[46]

Throughout the remainder of 2000, Palestinian residents of the occupied territories clashed with the IDF. By the end of the year, 279 Palestinians including 82 minors and 41 Israelis (no minors) had been killed in the unrest (B'Tselem, 2003b).

On 21 January 2001, Palestinian and Israeli delegates met President Clinton at Taba for further peace talks. Israel put forward an improved offer, but after a week Ehud Barak broke off the talks without an agreement, citing the nearness of the Israeli general election. Arafat condemned the decision to call off the talks, and accused Israel of waging 'a savage and barbaric war against the Palestinians'. Nevertheless both sides issued a statement stating that they had made progress and were closer to a deal than ever (*Guardian*, 29 January 2001). In an analysis of the talks Aronson claims that both sides moved closer on the territorial dimensions of a settlement. Israel dropped its demand for indefinite control of the Jordan Valley, the southern West Bank perimeter and area around Kiryat Arba, which comprised about 10 per cent of the West Bank (*Report on Israeli Settlements in the Occupied Territories*, March/April 2001). Instead their security concerns would have been met by 'the creation of discreet, limited security points in the Jordan Valley, arrangements which would have no territorial or settlement dimension and which would not be conditioned on Israeli control of principal transport routes'. There was also a reduction in Israeli demands for the annexation of the settlement corridors that protrude deeply into the prospective Palestinian state, breaking up territorial continuity, controlling roads and cantonising the territory. Aronson claimed that there still remained 'defects impacting upon both territorial continuity and transport corridors in crucial locations near Jerusalem, Ramallah, Bethlehem, Kalkilya and Nablus'.

The Palestinian negotiator Abu Ala put forward a map designed to overcome these. The map fulfilled three Palestinian territorial objectives: (1) 'reducing the area to be annexed by Israel to twice the settlements' current built-up areas; (2) minimizing the number of West Bank Palestinians in areas to be annexed by Israel from more than 20,000 projected by Israel's Taba map to practically zero; (3) rejecting the annexation of

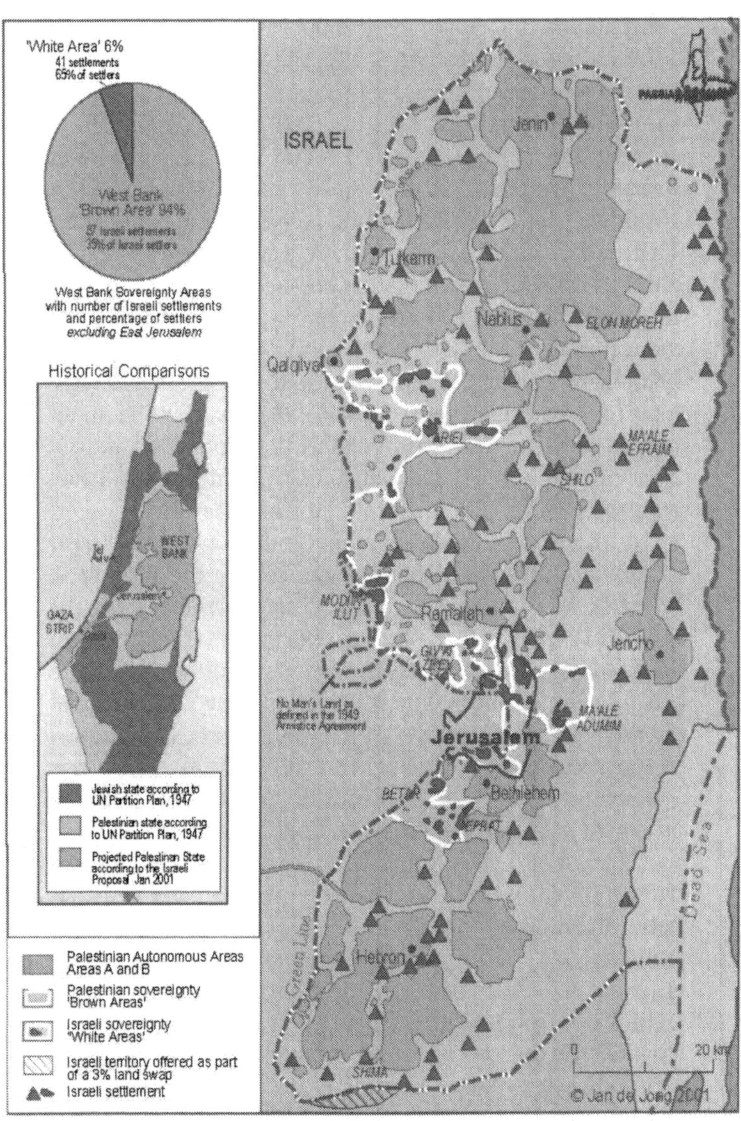

Map 7 Final Status Map presented by Israel, Taba, January 2001

any part of the Jerusalem area settlements of Ma'ale Adumim or Givat Ze'ev'. Aronson noted that the plan represented a 'historical and diplomatic landmark' in that it was the first official Palestinian proposal to accept Israeli annexation of part of the occupied territories. Dr Ron Pundak, the director of the Peres Centre for Peace in Tel-Aviv and a central figure in the Oslo process, claims that 'on the delicate issue of the Palestinian refugees and the right of return, the negotiators reached a draft determining the parameters and procedures for a solution, along with a clear emphasis that its implementation would not threaten the Jewish character of the State of Israel' (2001: 44). Pundak maintains that the talks had seen 'dramatic progress on all the most important issues' (2001: 44).

THE SHARON ADMINISTRATION

On 6 February 2001 Ariel Sharon won the Israeli election, pledging no negotiations with the Palestinians until the intifada ended. Exactly a week later Massoud Ayad, a member of Arafat's Force 17 bodyguards, was assassinated by an Israeli helicopter gunship, the first official killed since the assassination of the Fatah secretary and director general of the Palestinian Health Ministry, Thabet Thabet, on New Year's Eve. This killing had led to international condemnation because of Thabet's close association with Israeli peace activists (*Guardian*, 14 February 2001). On 19 February, Mahmud al-Madani, a young Hamas leader, was assassinated in Nablus. Shortly afterwards Israel's Labor party voted to join forces with Likud in a government of national unity, with Ariel Sharon as prime minister and Shimon Peres as foreign secretary. In early March, a Palestinian blew himself up in the coastal town of Netanya, killing three Israeli civilians and injuring 60 others, the first suicide attack within Israel since the beginning of the intifada.

The increasing violence led outside parties to try to intervene and stabilise the situation. On 27 March, the Non-Aligned States put forward a resolution (SC/7040) at the Security Council calling for a UN observer force to be dispatched to the occupied territories to protect Palestinian civilians. The resolution was vetoed by the United States, which cast the sole negative vote. The European Union also criticised the Israeli government for its 'disproportionate' use of force and called for it to end its illegal settlement of the occupied territories (*Guardian*, 22 May 2001). Such complaints were echoed by human rights groups who criticised Israel's use of helicopter gunships against civilians.

Throughout the summer of 2001 the violence continued. The Israelis launched a number of attacks on Palestinian towns and villages and continued to kill Palestinian political and military leaders, with 40 dying over the summer by rocket attacks from helicopter gunships. Palestinians and armed members of the Palestinian security services fought battles with the Israeli army. There were also a series of suicide bombings within Israel, the most deadly of which killed 19 young Israelis at the Dolphinarium Disco in Tel-Aviv on 1 June. This attack was immediately condemned by Amnesty International, who described the killing of the teenagers as 'shocking and reprehensible', adding that 'there can never be any justification for the targeting of civilians' (Amnesty International, 2001e). By the end of August 2001 154 Israelis (28 minors) and 495 Palestinians (123 minors) had been killed in the intifada (B'Tselem, 2003b).

After the 11 September 2001 attack on New York, Yasser Arafat met with Shimon Peres on 26 September in an attempt to reach a truce, but it failed to halt the bloodshed. Through the last months of 2001 the killings, suicide bombings, and Israeli attacks on Palestinian towns continued with heavy loss of life, particularly on the Palestinian side. On 16 October 2001 members of the Popular Front for the Liberation of Palestine killed the far right-wing Israeli minister Rehavam Ze'evi in a Jerusalem hotel room. The group claimed that this was in revenge for the killing of its leader by Israel on 27 August in a helicopter gunship attack. The killing of the Israeli minister who favoured the forced removal of all Palestinians from the West Bank and Gaza led to a strong rebuke from the White House, which stated that 'It is time for the Palestinian Authority to take vigorous action against terrorists, words are not enough' (Ari Fleisher, cited in the *Guardian*, 17 October 2005). The IDF then killed a number of Palestinian leaders and invaded Bethlehem, Ramallah, Nablus and Jenin where large numbers of Palestinian fighters and civilians, including many children, lost their lives. It also launched a number of airstrikes on Palestinian cities using F-16 jet fighters. Between September and December 2001 13 Israeli soldiers, 61 Israeli civilians (8 minors) and 241 Palestinian fighters and civilians (42 minors) were killed in the intifada.

The same pattern of violence continued throughout early 2002, reaching a peak in fatalities in March and April, with a number of suicide bombings inside Israel and the Israeli reoccupation of a number of West Bank towns including Nablus, Ramallah, Jenin and Bethlehem, where Palestinians had sought refuge in the Church of the Nativity after being pursued by the IDF. Yasser Arafat's compound in Ramallah was largely destroyed by tanks and bulldozers and the Palestinian leader was trapped under siege for four weeks. In March and April alone 66 Israeli soldiers, 100 Israeli civilians (13 minors) and 495 Palestinians (47 minors) were killed in the conflict. The invasion of Jenin proved extremely controversial, with initial Palestinian claims that a 'massacre' had taken place involving hundreds of civilians being subsequently criticised. Nevertheless the loss of life was very high: 23 Israeli soldiers and 57 Palestinians, of whom half were civilians, were killed and much of the Jenin refugee camp was destroyed.

Amnesty International produced a report on the Jenin and Nablus invasions, which examined allegations that the Israeli army indulged in 'unlawful killings', 'torture', the use of Palestinians as 'human shields' during military operations and the 'blocking of medical assistance, food and water; and the destruction of property', and concluded that:

> The IDF carried out actions which violated international human rights and humanitarian law, and that some of the actions amounted to grave breaches of the Fourth Geneva Convention relative to the Protection of Civilian Persons in Time of War of 1949 (the Fourth Geneva Convention) and were war crimes. (Amnesty International, 2002b)

The UN reported that the civilian death toll in the Israeli reoccupation of Nablus was twice as high as Jenin, and that in total 497 Palestinians were killed and 1,500 wounded between 1 March and 7 May 2002 (*Guardian*, 2 August 2002). July 2002 saw a particularly controversial incident when Israeli jets bombed a residential apartment block in Gaza city, killing Salah Shehada, the founder of Hamas's military wing as well as 15 other Palestinians, including nine children. The Israeli prime minister Ariel Sharon described it a 'great success', but the action was 'strongly condemned' by EU foreign policy chief Javier Solano. Criticism from the US was much milder, with White House spokesperson Ari Fleisher describing it as 'heavy-handed' (*Ha'aretz*, 23 July 2002).

In 2002, a group of Israeli combat officers and soldiers released a public statement detailing their unwillingness to serve in the occupied territories. The statement said that the 'price of the occupation' was 'the loss of IDF's human character and the corruption of the entire Israeli society' and that they would 'not continue to fight beyond the 1967 borders in order to dominate, expel, starve and humiliate an entire people' (*Ha'aretz*, 25 January 2002). This marked the establishment of the Seruv (Refuse) movement opposed to settlement-building and serving in the occupation of the Palestinian territories. The initial group was followed in September 2003 by a group of 27 elite combat pilots who in a separate letter stated that they would no longer carry out missions in the occupied territories: 'We, who have been educated to love the state of Israel refuse to take part in airforce attacks in civilian population centres. We refuse to continue harming innocent civilians' (*Guardian*, 25 September 2003).

In June 2002 Israel began construction of a wall that cut through the occupied territories. The Israeli government argued that the wall was necessary to stop the entry of suicide bombers into Israel. But Aronson suggests that the purpose of the wall is to create de facto borders in which Israel will absorb approximately 50 per cent of the West Bank, while Palestinians will be 'separated from each other and from Palestinian citizens of Israel by borders based upon settlement blocs' (*Report on*

Israeli Settlements in the Occupied Territories, July/August 2003). The Israeli human rights organisation B'Tselem (2003) has condemned the wall, which it projects will cause 'direct harm' to 210,000 Palestinians, turning some villages into 'isolated enclaves' and separating Palestinians from their farm lands, villages and livelihoods.

Also in June 2002 the US issued statements insisting that the Palestinians must replace their leader and reform their institutions before they would be granted a state. Speaking from Washington, President Bush stated that, 'When the Palestinian people have new leaders, new institutions and new security arrangements with their neighbors, the United States of America will support the creation of a Palestinian state.' He added that 'Peace requires a new and different Palestinian leadership so that a Palestinian state can be born.' This angered Palestinian negotiators, who questioned the right of the US to decide who the Palestinians could elect as their leader. The Palestinian negotiator, Saeb Erekat, argued that 'Palestinian leaders don't drop from parachutes from Washington or anywhere else. Palestinian leaders are chosen by the Palestinian people' (*Guardian*, 25 June 2002). The American statement effectively stated that the US administration would not publish its long-awaited 'road map' for peace until Arafat appointed a prime minister and delegated many of his powers. Finally, after further pressure, Yasser Arafat announced the make-up of a new cabinet in April 2003, with Mahmoud Abbas installed as Palestinian prime minister.

Shortly afterwards the Americans unveiled the 'Road Map', drawn up with input from the US, EU, UN and Russia. It called for the setting up of a Palestinian state in the West Bank and Gaza Strip by 2005. The plan had three stages. In the first the following should happen: all Palestinian violence must stop, Palestinian political structures must be reformed, Israel must dismantle the settlement outposts built since March 2001, and there must be a phased Israeli withdrawal from parts of the occupied territories. In the second stage, an international peace conference would take place and a provisional Palestinian state would come into being. The final stage would involve a solution to the most intractable issues such as borders, refugees and the status of Jerusalem. Arab states would also sign peace deals with Israel.

Soon thereafter, at the end of June 2003, Hamas, Islamic Jihad and Fatah called a three-month ceasefire to allow space for negotiation. However, the ceasefire did not hold in the face of further killings of Palestinian fighters and civilians by the IDF and a resumption of suicide bombings in Israel. As the killings on both sides escalated again, Mahmoud Abbas resigned as prime minister on 6 September after a brief and decisive power struggle with Yasser Arafat. His replacement, Ahmed Qureia, was sworn in the following day. The suicide bombings and killings of Palestinian leaders continued, and Israeli deputy Ehud Olmert publicly threatened to kill Yasser Arafat. This threat was condemned by the British government and some sections of the Israeli Knesset. The left-wing party Meretz argued that the Likud party was considering this as a strategy to prevent a two-state solution: 'If you deport Arafat you leave the ground only for Hamas, that's not something the government is doing out of stupidity. It's a strategy to keep things as they are, to prevent the solution of two states' (*Guardian*, 15 September 2003).

In October 2003, left-wing Israeli politicians and Palestinian leaders met to sign the 'Geneva Accords', an alternative vision for peace that specified in detail the parameters for a settlement of the conflict. This included a Palestinian state in almost all the West Bank and Gaza, the removal of the settlements, a right of return of Palestinian refugees to the future Palestinian state but not Israel, and the division of Jerusalem. The agreement received support from international leaders including Bill Clinton, but was condemned by the Israeli government. As 2003 drew to a close the construction of the West Bank wall was condemned by the European Union, UN General Assembly and UN Secretary General Kofi Annan. Between September and the end of January 2003 a further 25 Israeli soldiers, 36 Israeli civilians (5 minors) and 169 Palestinians (42 minors) were killed in violent incidents.

In early February 2004, in the midst of a corruption probe, Ariel Sharon shocked even members of his cabinet by announcing a plan to remove all the Jewish settlements from the Gaza Strip, on the basis that they were a security liability. The following month Israel killed the blind, quadriplegic spiritual leader of Hamas, Sheik Ahmed Yassin and three bystanders, with a multiple missile strike as he was taken to morning prayers at his local mosque in Gaza. Less than a month later his replacement as Hamas leader, the paediatrician Abdel Aziz Rantissi, was killed together with two aides by an Israeli missile strike on his car in Gaza. The attack was condemned by the European Union and the UN, but not the US, who stated that Israel had a right to defend itself. Shortly afterwards Ariel Sharon suggested that Israel might also kill Yasser Arafat. Meanwhile the suicide bombings and Israeli attacks on Palestinian towns and villages continued. Between March and May a further 16 Israeli soldiers, 17 Israeli civilians (4 minors) and 245 Palestinians (69 minors) were killed. Some of the worst loss of life occurred after the IDF invaded the Rafah refugee camp and caused extensive damage to properties. Eventually the IDF withdrew at the end of May 2004 after facing international criticism.

April 2004 also saw a seismic change in the official American approach to the conflict. For decades the official US approach had been to stick to the parameters of UN Resolution 242. The expectation was that Israel would withdraw to its pre-1967 borders and that a negotiated settlement would resolve the Palestinian 'right of return'. It was assumed that Israeli settlements in the occupied territories were 'an obstacle to peace'. However, on 14 April 2004, President Bush, flanked by Israeli Premier Ariel Sharon, announced a radical change in official policy by stating that 'in light of new realities on the ground, including already existing major Israeli population centers, it is unrealistic to expect that the outcome of final status negotiations will be a full and complete return to the armistice lines of 1949' (*Washington Post*, 15 April 2004). President Bush also rejected the right of return of Palestinians to Israel, stating that they should be resettled in a future Palestinian state.

The US move to legitimise Israel's key settlement blocks in the occupied territories and annul the 'right of return' for Palestinian refugees to Israel drew condemnation from Palestinian and European leaders. French President Jacques Chirac said that Bush's move had set an 'unfortunate and dangerous precedent' and rejected this change of policy. Similarly the Irish foreign minister, Brian Cowen, stated that 'the EU will not recognise any change to the pre-1967 borders other than those arrived at by agreement between the parties' (*Guardian*, 16 April 2004).

The BBC's Washington correspondent Jon Leyne suggested that it had angered the Palestinians because Washington had effectively 'pull[ed] the rug from under any future Palestinian negotiators by denying their demands before they have even begun talking'. He added that 'what concessions could a Palestinian negotiator now hope to get in return for renouncing the right of return, for example, when he knows Washington is already committed to opposing that principle?' Leyne suggested that Bush's change of policy was strongly influenced by America's pro-Israel lobby, which includes large numbers of Christian fundamentalists who are important backers of the Republican party:

> It looks as if he was flattened by 'The Bulldozer', as Mr Sharon is known. How could he be seen to be opposing the Israel lobby in this election year, after all? Yet the Israeli leader was pushing at an open door. In President Bush's black and white world, the Israelis are the good guys, the Palestinians, at least their leadership, are the villains ... Certainly Wednesday's announcement will be popular for Mr Bush back home as well, not just in the Jewish lobby, but also the Christian fundamentalists who make up a crucial part of his base, amongst hard line Republicans, and of course, amongst the Democrats, who won 90% of the Jewish vote in the last elections. (*BBC Online*, 14 April 2004)

Although the change in official US policy was condemned by many European leaders it was endorsed by Tony Blair, leading to an unprecedented condemnation by a coalition of 52 former British diplomats, who in an open letter argued that 'our dismay at this backward step is heightened by the fact that you yourself seem to have endorsed it, abandoning the principles which for nearly four decades have guided international efforts to restore peace in the Holy Land'. They added that 'there is no case for supporting policies which are doomed to failure' (*The Times*, 26 April 2004).

In July 2004, the International Court of Justice delivered its long-awaited verdict on the wall that Israel had been building deep into the occupied territories. The court ruled by 14 votes to one that the wall violated international law, with the American judge casting the sole dissenting vote. The ruling stated that the court was 'not convinced that the specific course Israel has chosen for the wall was necessary to attain its security objectives' and that its construction had led to the confiscation and destruction of large quantities of Palestinian property in contravention of the Fourth Geneva Convention. The ruling also reaffirmed the illegality of the Israeli settlements in the occupied territories and stated that there was a danger that construction of the wall 'would be tantamount to *de facto* (original emphasis) annexation' of parts of the occupied territories. The court stated that Israel should dismantle the wall and that it was 'under an obligation to make reparation for all damage caused by the construction of the wall in the Occupied Palestinian Territory'. The court also recommended that the UN General Assembly and Security Council should consider what action was required to force Israel to comply with the ruling.

The ruling was supported by the European Union but rejected by the Americans, who argued that disagreements about the wall should be resolved in bilateral negotiations between the Palestinians and Israelis. The Israelis argued that the International Court of Justice had no jurisdiction over the wall, that the ruling was unbalanced and failed to consider Israel's security concerns. The Israeli spokesperson Raanan Gissin stated that 'I believe that after all the rancour dies, this resolution will find its place in the garbage can of history. The court has made an unjust ruling denying Israel its right of self-defence' (*Guardian*, 10 July 2004).

In early October 2004, a storm of controversy erupted after one of Prime Minister's Sharon's closest aides, Dov Weisglass,

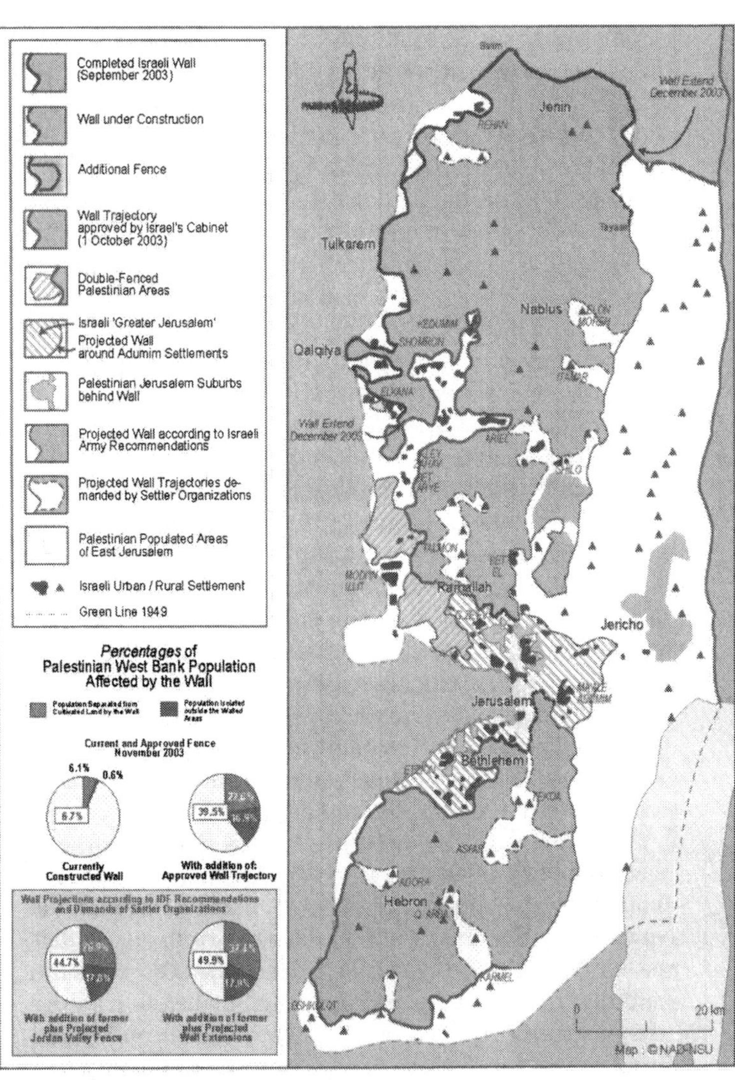

Map 8 The Wall in the West Bank, December 2003

gave an interview with *Ha'aretz* journalist Ari Shavit. In the interview Weisglass stated that at the end of 2003 the Israeli government had been worried about a series of current and future political developments. These included broad public support for the Geneva Accords, a stagnant economy, increasing numbers of high-profile 'refuseniks' and the possibility of future international pressure to reach a negotiated settlement with the Palestinians. Weisglass stated that the disengagement from Gaza would act as 'formaldehyde', which would freeze the road map 'so that there will not be a political process with the Palestinians':

> I found a device, in cooperation with the management of the world [the United States], to ensure that there will be no stopwatch here. That there will be no timetable to implement the settlers' nightmare. I have postponed that nightmare indefinitely. Because what I effectively agreed to with the Americans was that part of the settlements would not be dealt with at all, and the rest will not be dealt with until the Palestinians turn into Finns. That is the significance of what we did. The significance is the freezing of the political process. And when you freeze that process you prevent the establishment of a Palestinian state and you prevent a discussion about the refugees, the borders and Jerusalem. Effectively, this whole package that is called the Palestinian state, with all that it entails, has been removed from our agenda indefinitely. And all this with authority and permission. All with a presidential blessing and the ratification of both houses of Congress. What more could have been anticipated? What more could have been given to the settlers? (*Ha'aretz*, 8 October 2004)

On 29 October 2004, Yasser Arafat was suddenly taken ill and airlifted to a hospital in France where he died two weeks later. The significance of the death and legacy of Arafat who led the Palestinians for nearly four decades was disputed by politicians and commentators. Many in Israel were highly critical. Shimon Peres, with whom Arafat had shared the Nobel peace prize in 1994, stated that it is 'good that the world is rid of him ... the sun is shining in the Middle East' (*BBC Online*, 11 November 2004). The Israeli historian Michael Oren in a *Washington Post* article headlined 'Arafat without Tears:

The Terrorist Statesman Took Peace Nowhere' accused him of poisoning his own people's attitudes towards Israel and destroying the peace process:

> The arc of Arafat's image – from terrorist to Nobel Prize-winning peacemaker and back to terrorist – had been inscribed in the Israeli public's consciousness. Much of that public is now convinced that Arafat never intended to make peace, but merely used Oslo as a means of implementing the Palestinian Liberation Organization's 1974 'Phased Plan,' which called for Israel's gradual destruction through combined violence and diplomacy. Indeed, a solid majority of Israelis have come to believe that Arafat so poisoned his own people that, with or without him, there is little chance to renew negotiations, and that Israel's only option was to hunker down behind a fence separating Israelis from Palestinians until such time as the Palestinians produce a legitimate leadership capable of making peace. (*Washington Post*, 14 November 2004)

Alan Dershowitz, writing in the *Jerusalem Post*, offered an even harsher judgement on the Palestinian leader. He described Arafat as the 'godfather of international terrorism who dashed his people's hopes for statehood' and 'and indoctrinated [Palestinian] children with so much hatred that they willingly turned themselves into human bombs':

> Arafat was personally responsible for the murders of thousands of innocent Israelis, hundreds of innocent Americans, and countless others. Like other ethnically motivated butchers before him, he delighted in killing Jewish children, as he did in several well-planned attacks on Israeli schools and nurseries. He also personally ordered the murder of hundreds of his own people who disagreed with him or collaborated with Israel. Never a man to tolerate dissent, he employed bullets rather than arguments to respond to his critics. Arafat was the inspiration for Osama bin Laden, because he proved to his eager student that terrorism works and that terrorists can be praised and rewarded by a craven world, as Arafat was by so many for so long. Arafat was not one of those leaders who could, à la Nelson Mandela, make the transition from terrorist to peacemaker. He never learned how to take 'yes' for an answer and he never missed an opportunity to miss an opportunity. (*Jerusalem Post*, 12 November 2004)

However, not all Israelis offered such a damning critique of Arafat. Uri Avnery suggested that the Palestinian leader represented for most Israelis the personification of all the violence of the conflict, and for this reason they were unable to recognise the concessions and compromises he had made in trying to end the conflict:

> Every conflict generates massive amounts of stereotypes, prejudice, hate, and fear. All of the hate, fear and maybe the guilt, that we erected our national factory on the ruin of the Palestinian people. All of it focused on the character of Arafat. Millions of words condemning him have been written. I don't remember 100 words praising Arafat. It can not be that there does not exist any words of praise at all for a man. He was the initiator of Oslo, he recognized Israel. The man who gave up 77% of what was Palestine before 1948, and settled for 22% – there has to be something good in him. He was not portrayed as an enemy, but as a monster. He was portrayed as a great enemy and he could have been a great partner. (*Jerusalem Post*, 11 November 2004)

Some other commentators and political leaders offered positive evaluations of Arafat's life. Malaysian Prime Minister Abdullah Ahmad Badawi described him as a 'great leader' who would be remembered 'by people from all parts of the world for his courage and determination against all odds in championing and protecting the inalienable rights of the people of Palestine' (*BBC Online*, 11 November 2004). Former South African President Nelson Mandela described him as 'one of the outstanding freedom fighters of this generation, one who gave his entire life to the cause of the Palestinian people' (*BBC Online*, 11 November 2004). David Hirst, writing in the *Guardian*, offered a nuanced verdict on his life and legacy. He argued that Arafat had been vital in pulling the Palestinians together after the defeats of 1948 and 1967, but that his leadership after 1990 had been poor. Hirst criticised him for instituting torture and maltreatment in the Palestinian Authority and allowing his economic advisers to throw 'up a ramshackle, nepotistic edifice of monopoly, racketeering and naked extortion which enriched them as it further impoverished society at large'. Hirst, however, like Edward Said, reserved his strongest criticism for Arafat's decision to accept the parameters of the Oslo Accords, which he suggests were strongly weighted in Israel's favour and served to undermine Palestinian rights enshrined in international jurisprudence:

> He came as collaborator as much as liberator. Oslo provided for a series of 'interim' agreements leading to 'final-status' talks. An Israeli commentator said of the first of them: 'when one looks through all the lofty phraseology, all the deliberate disinformation, the hundreds of pettifogging sections, sub-sections, appendices and protocols, one clearly recognises that the Israeli victory was absolute and Palestine defeat abject.' It went on like this for six years, long after it had become obvious that his 'momentum' was working against, not for him. It had been bound to do so, because, in this dispensation that outlawed violence, spurned UN jurisprudence on the conflict, and consecrated a congenitally pro-Israeli US as sole arbiter of the peace process, the balance of power was more overwhelmingly in Israel's favour than ever. The 'interim' agreements which should have advanced his conception of 'final status' only advanced the Israelis' conception. (*Guardian*, 11 November 2004)

On 9 January 2005, the Palestinians in the occupied territories went to the polls and elected the Fatah candidate Mahmoud Abbas as president. Two weeks later, on 23 January, Hamas and Islamic Jihad agreed to suspend attack on Israel in order to give Abbas time to negotiate a ceasefire with the Israelis. This was eventually concluded on 8 February at Sharm el-Sheikh in Egypt, when Abbas met Ariel Sharon and agreed a ceasefire and terms for the Israelis to release Palestinian prisoners and move their troops out of Palestinian population centres. Hamas protested after the summit that it hadn't been properly consulted about the ceasefire but also declared that it wouldn't breach it without provocation. Despite the ceasefire the killings continued albeit at a lower rate. Between the ceasefire being signed in February and the Gaza disengagement in August a further 18 Israelis (4 minors) and 60 Palestinians (17 minors) were killed (B'Tselem, 2005).

In early August 2005, Israeli troops moved in to Gaza to remove the Israeli settlers who had refused to accept the government's compensation package and relocate voluntarily. Despite predictions of widespread violence and resistance all Israeli settlers were removed from the Gaza Strip within a matter of days without serious bloodshed. The reasons behind the disengagement from Gaza were the subject of much controversy. The British and American governments spoke of it as a step towards peace. The Israeli cabinet resolution that had authorised the disengagement stated that there was 'no reliable Palestinian partner with which it can make progress in a two-sided peace process' and that it would disengage from Gaza to achieve a 'a better security, political, economic and demographic situation' (Israeli Ministry of Foreign Affairs, 2004).

The demographic situation was considered to be particularly pressing. Haifa University geographer Arnon Soffer, who was widely seen as the originator of Ariel Sharon's separation plan, explained the nature of the demographic threat in a 2004 *Jerusalem Post* interview. He suggested that the deal the Israelis were offering to the Palestinians was so unacceptable that they would probably seek to wait until they comprised a majority in the area under Israeli control (Israel and the occupied territories) and then demand equal voting rights, a move that would threaten Israel's existence as a Jewish state. Removing the 1.3 million Palestinians from Israeli control in Gaza would put off that possibility for a number of years:

> Let's view it from a Palestinian perspective. Let's pretend you and I are Arafat and Yasser Abed Rabbo looking at the map. Look at what the Jews are going to leave us for a state. They're going to leave us the Gaza Strip – which is no more than a crowded 'prison'. Then there's another 'prison' called Hebron, and another, larger one called Samaria. Here there are 1.6 million, here 1 million, and here 1.5 million (soon to be 3 million). Each of these 'prisons' is cut off from the rest. The Jews won't permit us to have an army, while their own powerful army will surround us. They won't permit us to have an air force, while their own air force will fly over us. They won't allow us the Right of Return. Why should we make a deal with them? Why should we accept a state from them? Let's wait patiently for another 10 years, when

the Jews will comprise a mere 40 per cent of the country, while we will be 60 per cent. The world won't allow a minority to rule over a majority, so Palestine will be ours. (*Jerusalem Post*, 10 May 2004)

Soffer predicted a bleak and violent future after the disengagement from Gaza, although he also suggested that Israel's demographic and security situation would improve and a 'voluntary transfer' of Palestinians from the occupied territories might be achieved:

Instead of entering Gaza, the way we did last week, we will tell the Palestinians that if a single missile is fired over the fence, we will fire 10 in response. And women and children will be killed, and houses will be destroyed. After the fifth such incident, Palestinian mothers won't allow their husbands to shoot Kassams, because they will know what's waiting for them. Second of all, when 2.5 million people live in a closed-off Gaza, it's going to be a human catastrophe. Those people will become even bigger animals than they are today, with the aid of an insane fundamentalist Islam. The pressure at the border will be awful. It's going to be a terrible war. So, if we want to remain alive, we will have to kill and kill and kill. All day, every day. If we don't kill, we will cease to exist. (*Jerusalem Post*, 10 May 2004)

He also commented on the impact of those policies on Israeli society and the long-term effect on Palestinians:

The only thing that concerns me is how to ensure that the boys and men who are going to have to do the killing will be able to return home to their families and be normal human beings. The Palestinians will be forced to realize that demography is no longer significant, because we're here and they're there. And then they will begin to ask for 'conflict management' talks – not that dirty word 'peace.'... Unilateral separation doesn't guarantee 'peace' – it guarantees a Zionist-Jewish state with an overwhelming majority of Jews; it guarantees the kind of safety that will return tourists to the country; and it guarantees one other important thing. Between 1948 and 1967, the fence was a fence, and 400,000 people left the West Bank voluntarily. This is what will happen after separation. If a Palestinian cannot come into Tel Aviv for work, he will look in Iraq, or Kuwait, or London. I believe that there will be movement out of the area. (*Jerusalem Post*, 10 May 2004)

Graham Usher also notes what he sees as the key role of demography both in the withdrawal from Gaza and in Israel's naturalisation policies.

> Its only logic is demographic: the desperate fear that somehow without ending its presence in Gaza, Israel will one day find itself responsible for 1.3 million Palestinian residents. Demography is also the rationale behind Israel's new naturalisation policies. These grant citizenship to any Jew on the planet, but place draconian restrictions on citizenship on any Palestinians, in the occupied territories or elsewhere, who marry (in some cases, literally) their cousins inside Israel. In Kimmerling's phrase, this is '*herrenvolk*' law that is utterly unabashed about making ethnic discrimination and racial superiority the cornerstone of citizenship. Plans are already in place to expel thousands of 'illegal' Palestinians now in Israel 'across the border' once the border (that is, the wall) is built. (Usher, 2006: 20)

The Israeli withdrawal from Gaza was followed by a series of political earthquakes in the latter months of 2005. On 10 November, Shimon Peres was unexpectedly defeated for the leadership of the Labor party by Amir Peretz, a trade union leader who immediately indicated that he would pull Labor out of its National Unity coalition with Likud and trigger a general election. Peretz's victory was particularly surprising given that he was the first Sephardic Jew elected as leader of what is widely seen as an Ashkenazi-dominated party. Some in the party hoped that this might increase Labor's share of the vote among Middle Eastern Jews who traditionally favoured Likud. On 22 November, a new party Kadima ('Forward'), was formed which immediately attracted defections from both Likud and Labor, including senior figures such as Shimon Peres, Ehud Olmert and Shaul Mofaz. Early opinion polls suggested that Kadima would become the largest party in the general election scheduled for 28 March 2006. On 18 December, Ariel Sharon suffered a minor stroke, but was released from hospital soon afterwards. Two days later Binyamin Netanyahu was elected the new Likud leader, pledging not to give back any more Palestinian territory unless such moves were first approved by Israelis in a referendum. On 4 January 2006, Ariel Sharon suffered a second and much more devastating stroke which left him in a coma. His place as leader of the newly formed Kadima was taken up by his deputy Ehud Olmert.

At the end of January 2006, the Palestinians went to the polls in what was predicted to be closely fought parliamentary elections. In a surprise result Hamas not only triumphed over Fatah for the first time but actually gained a majority of seats, creating the possibility that it might form a government without coalition partners. The result was attributed by some to being a protest against the corruption of Fatah, or as a reaction to the failure of the international community to respond to legal ways of dealing with the conflict. This included most notably the absence of any international action on the ruling by the Court of Justice on the separation barrier. The reaction of Europe and the US to the election result was very negative, and they threatened to withdraw funding from the Palestinian Authority unless Hamas renounced violence and recognised the State of Israel. In the long term it is not possible to predict the outcome of these new developments. It may be that Palestinians led by Hamas will draw closer to countries such as Iran as they seek new sources of funding. In this future the period may be seen as a decisive moment in the radicalisation not just of Palestinians but of many other groups in the Muslim world.

History does not end, so in that sense there are no final words to be said here. We must simply halt our book at this moment in the unfolding of this very bitter conflict. In the account we have given, it was not our intention to take 'sides' or assert what the different parties should do. We sought to lay out all the competing arguments. In this we hope that our work contributes to a better-informed public debate about the causes of the conflict, what solutions are possible and what may be done to achieve them.

Notes

1. In a letter dated 24 October 1915 McMahon laid out the areas in which Britain planned to grant independence: 'The two districts of Mersina and Alexandretta and portions of Syria lying west of the districts of Damascus, Homs, Hama and Aleppo cannot be said to be purely Arab, and should be excluded from the limits demanded. With the above modification, and without prejudice to our existing treaties with Arab chiefs we accept those limits. As for the regions lying within those frontiers wherein Britain is free to act without detriment to the interests of her ally, France, I am empowered in the name of the Government of Great Britain to give the following assurances and make the following reply to your letter: (1) Subject to the above modifications, Great Britain is prepared to recognize and support the independence of the Arabs in all the regions within the limits demanded by the Sharif of Mecca' (letter cited in Ingrams, 1972: 2).
2. According to the British census of 1922, the total population of Palestine was 752,048, comprised of 83,790 Jews, 589,177 Muslims and 71,464 Christians (United Nations, 1945).
3. In a memorandum to Lord Curzon on 11 August 1919, Balfour wrote: 'the contradiction between the letters of the Covenant and the policy of the Allies is even more flagrant in the case of the "independent nation" of Palestine than in that of the "independent nation" of Syria. For in Palestine we do not propose even to go through the form of consulting the wishes of the present inhabitants of the country, though the American [King–Crane] Commission has been going through the form of asking what they are' (British Government, Foreign Office, 1919b, cited in Ingrams, 1972: 73).
4. The Revisionist movement was a political rival of Ben-Gurion's Labor movement. It espoused a more militant attitude towards the Arabs and a more liberal economic policy. Much of its support in the 1920s and 1930s came from Polish immigrants. The Revisionists laid claim to all of Palestine and Transjordan and

argued that conflict with the Arabs was inevitable. The military wing Betar was formed in the 1920s. Some Betar members split away in the 1930s to form the Irgun paramilitary group who fought the British mandatory authorities in the 1940s. The Revisionist movement later provided much of the constituency for the Herut and Likud parties.

5. The Oxford historian Albert Hourani described Joan Peters's book as 'ludicrous and worthless' in *The Observer*. Ian and David Gilmour called it 'preposterous' in the *London Review of Books*. *Time Out* described it as a 'piece of disinformation roughly the size and weight of a dried cowpat', while the chair of the Philosophy Department at the Hebrew University, Avishai Margalit, condemned Peters's 'web of deceit' (reviews cited in Finkelstein, 2001: 45–6). McCarthy argues that unrecorded Arab immigration into Palestine during the Mandate period was 'small' and that for it to 'have had a significant effect on the ethnic composition of Palestine it would have had to have been immense'. He concludes that the 'argument that Arab immigration somehow made up a large part of the Palestinian Arab population is thus statistically untenable' (1990: 34). For a discussion of the effects of improvements in sanitation and hygiene on population increase in Palestine, see Friedlander & Goldscheider (1979).
6. Gilbert claims that in 1943 the British authorities at Churchill's behest relaxed the bar on Jewish immigration into Palestine by allowing 'any refugee who could get by rail or sea, out of the Balkans to Istambul [to] proceed to Palestine regardless of existing quotas' (1999: 115). He estimates that several thousand took this route.
7. The US Secretary of State, James Byrnes, wrote to the British Foreign Secretary, Lord Halifax, arguing that American Jewry was not interested in the plight of the refugees in Europe, their main concern being that Jews 'ought to have a country to call their own'. Harold Beeley in the British Foreign Office complained that 'the Zionists have been deplorably successful in selling the idea that even after the Allied victory immigration to Palestine represented for many Jews "their only hope of survival"' (both cited in Ovendale, 1999: 94).
8. The pressure to open up Palestine to the Jewish refugees worried the British, who feared the impact on public order. Ovendale

(1999) claims that the US War Department had estimated that it would have to send 300,000 troops to Palestine to keep the peace if the area was opened to Jewish immigration. He also suggests that the US State Department was also concerned that an Arab backlash would strengthen Russian influence in a vital geostrategic area and recommended that the British colonial empire be maintained intact.

9. For a comprehensive overview of the case put forward by the Arab delegates, see the Official Records of the General Assembly, Second Session, Ad Hoc Committee on the Palestine Question, pp. 276–9, cited in UN, 1990.
10. The Philippines, Haiti and Colombia all spoke out against the partition resolution, but at the last minute changed their position, with the Philippines and Haiti supporting the resolution and Colombia abstaining.
11. A number of delegates including Lebanese representatives claimed during debates at the UN that representatives from the US and USSR had used bribes and threats of economic sanctions in order to coerce smaller states to vote for the partition of Palestine (Official Records of the General Assembly, Second Session, Plenary Meetings, vol. II, 124th meeting: 1310).
12. For an overview of the concept of transfer in Zionist thinking, see Masalha (1992). This perspective is challenged by Karsh (2000).
13. In 1959 the Palestinian historian Walid Khalidi went through the official records of Arab governments as well as Arab newspapers and the radio monitoring reports of the BBC and CIA, and could find no evidence of broadcasts urging Palestinians to flee. This research was also independently corroborated by the Irish scholar Erskine Childers in 1961. For an overview and discussion of the controversy, see Hitchens & Said (1988). Some historians such as Gilbert (1999) argue that many Arabs left voluntarily prior to the arrival of the Arab armies in May 1948 without mentioning the impact of the alleged broadcasts.
14. This position is supported by Shlaim who points to an array of underlying political and geopolitical rivalries, which were camouflaged by claims that the Arab states were acting to defend the Palestinians in the spirit of pan-Arab unity: 'Dynastic rivalries played a major part in shaping Arab approaches to Palestine. King Abdullah of Transjordan was driven by a long-standing ambition

to make himself the master of Greater Syria which included, in addition to Transjordan, Syria, Lebanon, and Palestine. King Faruq saw Abdullah's ambition as a direct threat to Egypt's leadership in the Arab world. The rulers of Syria and Lebanon saw in King Abdullah a threat to the independence of their countries and they also suspected him of being in cahoots with the enemy. Each Arab state was moved by its own dynastic or national interests. Arab rulers were as concerned with curbing each other as they were in fighting the common enemy. Under these circumstances it was virtually impossible to reach any real consensus on the means and ends of the Arab intervention in Palestine. Consequently, far from confronting a single enemy with a clear purpose and a clear plan of action, the Yishuv faced a loose coalition consisting of the Arab League, independent Arab states, irregular Palestinian forces, and an assortment of volunteers. The Arab coalition was one of the most divided, disorganized, and ramshackle coalitions in the entire history of warfare' (Shlaim, 2005).

15. Shlaim suggests that Ben-Gurion was very keen for Israel to develop its own nuclear weapons, and the supply of French nuclear technology was a significant factor in encouraging Israel to join the French and British in their attack on Egypt. Recently discovered British government files also revealed that Britain played an important role in facilitating Israel's development of nuclear weapons by supplying Israel with heavy water (*Guardian*, 4 August 2005).
16. This controversial incident has been the subject of much debate. The Israeli authorities have always maintained that it was a 'tragic case of misidentification'. Bregman (2003: 120–2) notes that others have suggested that it was deliberately undertaken to prevent the *Liberty* from detecting Israeli troop concentrations massing in Galilee as part of the next day's attack on the Golan Heights. He argues that recently declassified tapes of conversations between airforce personnel support the conclusion that the attack on the American ship was deliberate.
17. Yitzak Rabin remarked after Israel's victory that 'I do not believe that Nasser wanted war. The two divisions that he sent into Sinai on May 14 would not have been enough to unleash an offensive against Israel. He knew it and we knew it' (*Le Monde*, 29 February 1968, cited in Hirst, 1977: 211). In a 1982 speech at the National

Defense College Menachem Begin stated that 'The Egyptian Army concentrations in the Sinai do not prove that Nasser was really about to attack us. We must be honest with ourselves. We decided to attack him' (*New York Times*, 21 August 1982).

18. Menachem Begin claimed that in the penultimate Ministerial Committee on Defence prior to the war military leaders 'had no doubt of victory' and 'expressed their belief not only in the strength of the army but also in its ability to rout the enemy' (Begin, cited in Finkelstein, 2001: 135) The former Commander of the Israeli Air Force Ezer Weizman has claimed in relation to the 1967 War that 'there was no threat of destruction to the State of Israel' but that the war was justified so that Israel could 'exist according to the scale, spirit and quality she now embodies' (*Ha'aretz*, 29 March 1972, cited in Chomsky, 1999: 100).
19. Norman Finkelstein (2001) alleges that Marshall Tito of Yugoslavia put forward a peace plan involving a full Israeli withdrawal from the occupied territories in exchange for 'full demilitarization and other security guarantees in the evacuated territories', as well as an 'end to the call for an Arab state of Palestine'. He alleges that this proposal was accepted by both Egypt and Jordan but rejected by Israel as 'one-sided'.
20. The British representative, Lord Caradon, denied any ambiguity in the interpretation of 242, claiming that 'in our resolution we stated the principle of the "withdrawal of Israeli armed forces from territories occupied in the recent conflict" and in the preamble emphasized "the inadmissibility of the acquisition of territory by war". In our view the wording of the provisions is clear.' The French delegate emphasised that 'on the point which the French delegation has always stressed as being essential – the question of the withdrawal of the occupation forces – the resolution which has been adopted, if we refer to the French text which is equally authentic with the English, leaves no room for any ambiguity, since it speaks of withdrawal "des territoires occupes", which indisputably corresponds to the expression "occupied territories". The Indian representative asserted that "the principle of the inadmissibility of territorial acquisition by force is absolutely fundamental to our approach" and "it is our understanding that the draft resolution, if approved by the Council, will commit it to the application of the principle of total withdrawal of Israeli forces

from all of the territories – I repeat, all the territories – occupied by Israel as a result of the conflict which began on 5 June 1967"' (all cited in Finkelstein, 2001: 146).

21. Finkelstein points to the memoirs of the American diplomat Dean Rusk who claimed that the United States favoured omitting the definite article in the withdrawal clause because 'we thought the Israeli border along the West Bank could be "rationalised", certain anomalies could easily be straightened out with some exchanges of territory, making a more sensible border for all parties'. (Rusk, 1991: 388–9, cited in Finkelstein, 2001: 148). However, he stressed 'we never contemplated any significant grant of territory to Israel as a result of the June 1967 war. On that point we and the Israelis to this day remain sharply divided' (Rusk, 1991: 388–9, cited in Finkelstein, 2001: 148).
22. See, for instance, Efrain Karsh, 'What Occupation?', *Commentary*, July 2002 or Max Singer, 'Right is Might', *Jerusalem Post*, 29 June 1997.
23. Chomsky points to an article by Yedidia Segal in the 3 September 1982 issue of *Nekudah*, the journal of the religious West Bank settlers, which stated that 'those among us who call for a humanistic attitude towards our [Arab] neighbours are reading the Halacha [religious law] selectively and are avoiding specific commandments'. Segal argues that the gentiles are 'a people like a donkey' and that the scriptures insist that 'conquered' peoples must 'serve' their Jewish masters and must be kept 'degraded and low' and 'must not raise their heads in Israel but must be conquered beneath their hand ... with complete submission'. 'There is no relation', Segal insists, 'between the law of Israel and atheistic modern humanism'. He cites Maimonides that 'in a divinely-commanded war [such as the 1982 Lebanon invasion] one must destroy, kill and eliminate men, women and children', there being 'no place for any humanistic considerations' (cited in Chomsky, 1999: 123–4).
24. UN General Assembly Resolution 54/37, adopted 1 December 1999.
25. Hirst claims that 'In Israel's Arab schools children have always had to see their own Arab culture, history and religion through Israeli eyes: they saw it deliberately mocked and falsified. Arab history became little more than a series of revolutions, murders,

feuds and plunderings, whilst everything in the Jewish past was ennobled and glorified. It was always the Arabs in decline they learned about, never in their greatness; the heroes of the past, the Prophet, the Caliph Harun al-Rashid and Saladin, got perfunctory mention. In four years of secondary education Arab children had 384 periods of Jewish history as against only 32 of their own. The study of Old Testament was compulsory, while the Muslim and Christian religions were not taught at all' (1977: 238).

26. For instance, General Assembly Resolution 53/56, passed 3 December 1998 by 151 votes to 2; Resolution 52/67, passed 10 December 1997 by 151 to 2; Resolution 51/134, passed 13 December 1996 by 149 votes to 2; Resolution 49/36C, passed 9 December 1994 by 145 votes to 2; Resolution 47/70D, passed 14 December 1992 by 142 votes to 2.
27. In the late 1970s a *Sunday Times* report (19 June 1977) found that torture was so widespread and systematic that 'it appears to be sanctioned at some level as deliberate policy', perhaps 'to persuade Arabs in the occupied territories that it is least painful to behave passively'. More recently Amnesty International has issued annual reports cataloguing the use of torture by the Israeli authorities (e.g. Amnesty International, 2001a, 2000, 1998, 1997). A report (Amnesty International, 1999a) entitled *Flouting UN Obligations in the Name of Security* concluded that Israeli 'interrogation methods, such as violent shaking, or hooding, and shackling detainees to low chairs with loud music playing, constituted torture or cruel, inhuman or degrading treatment or punishment and thus contravened Article 1 of the Convention against Torture' and that torture is 'officially authorized at the highest level and indeed effectively legalized'. In the same report it was noted that the 1,600 Palestinians detained by Israeli security forces in 1998 were 'routinely tortured or ill-treated during interrogation'. The *Independent* journalist Robert Fisk has produced a number of reports from the Israeli-controlled Khiam detention centre in Southern Lebanon detailing the use of electric shock torture applied to the genitals (*Independent*, 20 May 2000). A BBC *Correspondent* documentary (4 November 2000) also reported from Khiam, claiming that torture had also been used against children and pregnant women, and that prisoners had been tortured to death, in what Amnesty International described as 'war crimes'.

28. The use of 'administrative detention' involved detaining Palestinians for long periods without trial or legal recourse. In the 1970s Hirst alleges that many Palestinians suspected of involvement with opposition movements were interned in camps in the desert: 'At its worst it meant the establishment of veritable concentration camps buried in remote corners of the Sinai desert. Nakhl, Abu Zu'aiman, Kusseimah were the names of places where whole families were kept in isolation from the outside world. They were there because relatives of theirs were suspected, no more, of working for the resistance. Crowded into tents surrounded by barbed wire, they were denied radios, newspapers or the most basic amenities from their homes, which were frequently destroyed during their captivity. Women and children would be put in one camp, male relatives of "wanted persons" – brother, nephews, cousins – in another' (1977: 248). By 1980 the Israeli daily *Ha'aretz* estimated the number of security prisoners or detainees passing through Israeli jails since 1967 at close to 200,000 people or 20 per cent of the population, leading to a situation of 'horrendous overcrowding' and 'appalling human suffering and corruption' (8 August 1980, cited in Chomsky, 1999: 128). For more recent reports on detention without trial, see Amnesty International (1999a).
29. Collective punishment could involve curfews where the local population is not allowed out for more than an hour or two a day for weeks or months at a time, schools are closed and there is no employment. Israel has justified the use of curfews on the basis that confining the Palestinian population to their homes for long periods prevents militants from attacking Jews. The use of collective punishment is illegal under international law, and Israel has drawn repeated censure from the UN: 'The United Nations Commission on Human Rights calls upon Israel to cease immediately its policy of enforcing collective punishments, such as demolition of houses and closure of the Palestinian territory, measures which constitute flagrant violations of international law and international humanitarian law, endanger the lives of Palestinians and also constitute a major obstacle in the way of peace' (United Nations, 1999). A report by the Israeli journalist Aharon Bachar in the Israeli daily *Yediot Ahornot* described a meeting where Labor Alignment leaders presented Menachem

Begin with 'detailed accounts of terrorist acts [against Arabs] in the conquered territories'. They described the collective punishment in the town of Halhul where: 'The men were taken from their houses beginning at midnight, in pyjamas, in the cold. The notables and other men were concentrated in the square of the mosque and held there until morning. Meanwhile men of the border guards broke into houses beating people with shouts and curses. During the many hours that hundreds of people were kept in the mosque square, they were ordered to urinate and excrete on one another and also to sing Hatikva [Jewish National Anthem] and to call out "Long Live the State of Israel". Several times people were beaten and ordered to crawl on the ground. Some were even ordered to lick the earth. At the same time four trucks were commandeered and at daybreak, the inhabitants were loaded onto the trucks, about 100 in each truck, and taken like sheep to the Administration headquarters in Hebron' (3 December 1982, cited in Chomsky, 1999: 131). The report further alleged that prisoners were beaten, tortured and humiliated and that settlers were permitted into prisons to take part in the beatings. For more recent reports on collective punishments, see Amnesty International (2001b, 2001c) or Human Rights Watch (1996).

30. Hirst cites evidence from the Israeli League for Civil and Human Rights that searches 'were often carried with great brutality and violence'. During night-time raids, Hirst claims that it was a 'regular practice to ... carry men off to prison without any good reason, beat them up and torture them' (1977: 249).
31. The suspicion that the concept of the 'Democratic State of Palestine' was not sincere was reinforced by the fact that the Palestinian National Council failed to produce an amendment to the Palestinian National Charter, which would have specified that all the Jews in Palestine (not just those after a specified date such as 1917 or 1948) would have been entitled to Palestinian citizenship (Hirst, 1977).
32. After 1967 there were numerous diplomatic efforts to break the deadlock, all of which were fruitless. King Hussein issued a six-point peace plan in early 1969 at the National Press Club in Washington. Speaking officially in conjunction with Egypt's Nasser, Hussein offered a comprehensive peace treaty and recognition of Israel in exchange for 'the withdrawal of its armed forces from all territories

occupied in the June 1967 war, and the implementation of all the other provisions of the Security Council Resolution (242)', adding that 'Israel may have either peace or territory – but she can never have both' (*Washington Report on Middle East Affairs*, 2 April 1984). This proposal was rejected by Israel. In December 1969 the American Secretary of State William Rogers put forward another peace agreement based on UN Resolution 242, specifying that Israel would return to the pre-1967 borders (with minor border modifications) and a solution to the Palestinian refugee problem would have to be found, in exchange for a comprehensive peace treaty. The proposals were rejected by the Israeli cabinet, who declared that 'if these proposals were carried out, Israel's security and peace would be in grave danger. Israel will not be sacrificed to by any power policy, and will reject any attempt to impose a forced solution upon it' (cited in Shlaim, 2000: 291). In 1971, the Swedish diplomat Dr Gunnar Jarring reported that Egypt had offered Israel a full peace treaty based on Resolution 242, with the stipulation that Israel also had to withdraw from the Sinai and Gaza Strip, settle the refugee problem in line with UN resolutions, and establish a UN force to keep the peace. Israel's reply, though positive, insisted that 'Israel will not return to the pre-5 June 1967 lines' (Shlaim, 2000: 300). This, Shlaim suggests, doomed the Jarring initiative (2000). It also drew repeated criticism from the United Nations. The Jarring initiative was followed by attempts at achieving an interim solution, which Shlaim suggests floundered on Israel's refusal to accept a timetable for a permanent settlement, and its desire for territorial revisionism. There followed in 1972 and 1973 a number of openly annexationist pronouncements by Israeli leaders. Moshe Dayan told *Time* magazine in July 1973 'there is no more Palestine. Finished', and in an April 1973 interview he talked of 'a new state of Israel with broad frontiers, strong and solid, with the authority of the Israeli government extending from the Jordan to the Suez Canal' (both cited in Shlaim, 2000: 316). Shlaim suggests that this, together with the later publication of the Galilee document detailing a large expansion of settlement-building in the occupied territories, left Sadat little choice but to use force to try to regain the Sinai.

33. Boyle (2002) argues that when the Israeli forces started advancing, the Soviets had considered inserting their own force into the

conflict, leading the Americans to raise their nuclear alert to Def Con Three, the highest state of preparedness. He claims that in the face of this the Soviets backed down but that the world had come perilously close to a nuclear confrontation between the superpowers. Three Israeli and American analysts have also claimed that Israel threatened to use nuclear weapons against Egypt, and in fact prepared to do so at the beginning of the 1973 War. This was in order to force America to provide a large consignment of conventional weapons, which was forthcoming (Perlmutter, Handel & Bar-Joseph, 1982).

34. In March 1977, the Palestinian National Council called for an 'independent national state' in Palestine and an Arab–Israeli peace conference. Prime Minister Rabin's reply was that 'the only place the Israelis could meet the Palestinian guerillas was on the field of battle' (*New York Times*, 21 March 1977). In 1977, the PLO leaked a 'peace plan' in Beirut that stated that the (explicitly rejectionist) Palestinian National Covenant would not serve as the basis for inter-state relations and that any progression beyond a two state-solution 'would be achieved by peaceful means' (*Manchester Guardian Weekly*, 7 August 1977). In November 1978, Tillman claims that Yasser Arafat in requesting a dialogue with American representatives issued the following statement: 'The PLO will accept an independent Palestinian state consisting of the West Bank and Gaza, with connecting corridor, and in that circumstance will renounce any and all violent means to enlarge the territory of the state. I would reserve the right, of course, to use non-violent means, that is to say diplomatic and democratic means, to bring about the eventual unification of all Palestine ... we will give de facto recognition to the State of Israel' (Tillman, 1982: 215–18). In April 1981, after PLO acceptance of the Soviet peace plan, the PLO representative Issam Sartawi declared that 'from this it follows that the PLO has formally conceded to Israel, in the most unequivocal manner, the right to exist on a reciprocal basis'. A week later Sartawi issued a joint statement with the former Israel general Mattityahu Peled: 'the PLO has made its willingness to accept and recognize the state of Israel on the basis of mutual recognition of each nation's legitimate right of self-determination crystal clear in various resolutions since 1977' (all references cited in Chomsky, 1999: 68–78).

35. Testimony of Dr Chris Giannou before the House Sub-committee on Europe and the Middle East, 13/7/1982 (cited in Chomsky, 1999: 229).
36. For other reports on ill treatment of detainees, see *Der Spiegel*, 14 March 1983; *Haolam Haze*,15 December 1982; or *The Times*, 18 March 1983.
37. On the subject of Palestinian weaponry, see Ze'ev Schiff (*Ha'aretz*, 18 July 1982) or Hirsh Goodman (*Jerusalem Post*, 9 July 1982), who suggested the Palestinian 'army' and weapons posed no significant threat to Israel and that many of the claims regarding the scale of weaponry were exaggerated. With regard to ceasefire violations the *Christian Science Monitor* (18 March 1982) reported that the PLO had observed the ceasefire despite many Israeli provocations. The Abu Nidal group, who attempted to assassinate the Israeli ambassador, were sworn enemies of the PLO leadership and had previously tried to assassinate Yasser Arafat. (All above references cited in Chomsky, 1999: 210.)
38. All extracts taken from *Do Not Say That You Did Not Know*, a report by the Israeli Committee for Solidarity with Bir Zeit, 5 June 1982 (cited in Chomsky, 1999: 60).
39. See, for instance, Report of the Special Committee to Investigate Israeli Practices Affecting the Human Rights of the Population of the Occupied Territories, A/RES/38/79, 15 December 1983 or Special Committee to Investigate Israeli Practices Affecting the Human Rights of the Population of the Occupied Territories, A/RES/39/95, 14 December 1984 or UN Commission on Human Rights: Question of the Violation of Human Rights in the Occupied Arab Territories, including Palestine, E/CN.4/RES/1985/1, 19 February 1985.
40. A B'Tselem (Israeli human rights group) report on the treatment of children detained by Israeli forces found that 'illegal violence against minors ... many [of whom] are innocent of any crime ... occurs on a large scale'. It found that violence directed against minors including 'slapping, punching, kicking, hair pulling, beatings with clubs or with iron rods, pushing into walls and onto floors' was 'very common'. It also detailed more severe forms of ill treatment: 'Beating the detainee as he is suspended in a closed sack covering the head and tied around the knees; tying the detainee in a twisted position to an outdoor pipe with

hands behind the back for hours and, sometimes, in the rain, at night, and during the hot daytime hours; confining the detainee, sometimes for a few days, in the "lock-up" – a dark, smelly and suffocating cell one and a half by one and a half meters [five by five feet]; placing the detainee, sometimes for many hours, in the "closet" – a narrow cell the height of a person in which one can stand but not move; and depositing the tied-up detainee for many hours in the "grave" – a kind of box, closed by a door from the top, with only enough room to crouch and no toilet.' The Israeli daily *Hotam* (1 April 1988) reported the beating of a ten-year-old during an army interrogation who was left 'looking like a steak', noting that soldiers 'weren't bothered' when they later found out that the boy was deaf-mute and mentally retarded. Reporting on the treatment of Palestinians as young as fourteen arrested 'on suspicion of stone throwing', the Israeli daily *Hadashot* (24 February 1992) cited the testimony of an insider at the Hebron detention centre: 'What happened there ... was plain horror: they would break their clubs on the prisoners' bodies, hit them in the genitals, tie a prisoner up on the cold floor and play soccer with him – literally kick and roll him around. Then they'd give him electric shocks, using the generator of a field telephone, and then push him out to stand for hours in the cold and rain.... They would crush the prisoners ... turning them into lumps of meat'. (All above reports cited in Finkelstein, 1996: 47–9.)

41. For other references on Hezbullah's influence on Hamas, see *Ha'aretz* (21 April 1994) or *Nida' al-Watan* (15 November 1996).
42. Among others the poet Mahmoud Darwish, the PLO's Lebanon representative Shafiq al-Hut (both of whom resigned from the PLO executive committee in protest), the leader of the Palestinian negotiating team and Gaza Red Crescent Society, Haidar Abd al-Shafi, the Palestinian negotiator as well as other prominent Fatah and PLO officials.
43. Hezbullah, which also runs a network of social services, claims it is trying to protect the local population, many of whom have been expelled from their home by Israel's proxy force in the South Lebanon. Human rights groups have condemned the expulsions as 'war crimes' and demanded that they stop (Human Rights Watch, 1999). The organisation has also condemned both Israel and Hezbullah for targeting civilians.

44. The day before the agreement was signed Human Rights Watch (1998) urged the United States and Israel not to pressurise the Palestinian Authority to expand its security crackdown without all sides making a clear commitment to safeguard human rights. Human Rights Watch pointed out that the 'Palestinian Authority's human rights record is already deplorable', and that the 'U.S. doesn't condemn these violations now – will the U.S. condemn violations once it is formally part of the process that creates them?' The Israeli human rights group B'Tselem published a report a month after the signing, pointing to 'mass arbitrary arrests by both the Palestinian Authority and Israel', and alleging that 'the agreement merely pays lip service to human rights, with no intention by any of the parties – Israel, the Palestinian National Authority or the United States – to hold the sides accountable for human rights violations'.
45. Barak claimed that he would not allow the Syrians to reach the waters of the River Tiberias (where Israel draws much of its water); the Syrians claimed that Barak was trying to lure them into an 'Arafat-style agreement, normalize relations, curb Hezbullah and then we might withdraw'.
46. See, for instance, Conal Urquhart's article 'Israeli soldiers tell of indiscriminate killings by army and a culture of impunity' (*Guardian*, 6 September 2005).

References

Aham, A. (1923) *Am Scheideweg* (Berlin)

Amnesty International. (2002a) 'Without Distinction: Attacks on Civilians by Palestinian Armed Groups'. AI Index: MDE 02/003/2002

—— (2002b) 'Israel and the Occupied Territories: Shielded from Scrutiny: IDF Violations in Jenin and Nablus'. AI Index: MDE 15/149/2002

—— (2001a) 'Annual Report 2001 Israel and the Occupied Territories'. AI Index: POL 10/001/2001

—— (2001b) 'Israel/OT: The International Community Must Act to end Israel's Policy of Closures and House Demolitions'. AI Index: MDE 15/066/2001

—— (2001c) 'Israel/OT: Committee Against Torture says Israel's Policy of Closures and Demolitions of Palestinian Homes May Amount to Cruel Inhuman or Degrading Treatment'. AI Index: MDE 15/105/2001

—— (2001d) 'Israel/OT: Annual Report'. AI Index: POL 10/001/2001

—— (2001e) 'Israel/OT/Palestinian Authority: Amnesty International Condemns Bombing of Discotheque'. AI Index: MDE 15/049/2001

—— (2000) 'Annual Report 2001 Israel and the Occupied Territories'. AI Index: POL 10/001/00

—— (1999a) 'Israel: Flouting UN Obligations in the Name of Security. Oral Statement to the UN Commission on Human Rights on Israel and the Occupied Territories'. AI Index: MDE 15/034/1999

—— (1999b) 'Israel and the Occupied Territories: Demolition and Dispossession: the Destruction of Palestinian Homes'. AI Index: MDE 15/059/1999

—— (1998) 'Annual Report 1998 Israel and the Occupied Territories'. AI Index: POL 10/001/1998

—— (1997) 'Annual Report 1997 Israel and the Occupied Territories'. AI Index: POL 10/001/1997

—— (1996a) 'Israel/Lebanon Unlawful Killings during Operation Grapes of Wrath'. AI Index: MDE 15/042/1996

—— (1996b) 'Israel/Lebanon: Amnesty International Demands Effective Protection for Civilians, Calls for Proper Enquiry into Killings by Israel'. AI Index: MDE 15/049/1996

Bard, M. (2003) *Myths and Facts Online Israel and Lebanon* [Internet]. Available from: <http://www.us-israel.org/jsource/myths/mf11.html> [Accessed 6 September 2003]

Bauer, Y. (1970) *Flight and Rescue: Brichah* (New York: Random House)

Beilin, Y. (1985) *Mehiro Shel Ihud* (in Hebrew) (Revivim)

Bohm, A. (1935) *Die Zionistische Bewegung* (Berlin)

Boyle, W.J. (2002) *The Two O'Clock War: The 1973 Yom Kippur Conflict and the Airlift that Saved Israel* (New York: St Martins Press)

Bregman, A. (2003) *A History of Israel* (Basingstoke: Palgrave Macmillan)

British Government (1947) 'The Political History of Palestine under the British Administration' (Memorandum to the United Nations Special Committee on Palestine), Jerusalem

—— (1939) 'Report of a Committee on Correspondence between Sir Henry McMahon and the Sherif of Mecca', Parliamentary Papers, Cmd. 5974

—— (1930) 'Palestine: Report on Immigration, Land Settlement and Development', Cmd. 3686

—— (1919a) Public Record Office. Foreign Office No. 800/215

—— (1919b) Public Record Office. Foreign Office No. 371/4183

B'Tselem (2003a) *Casualty Statistics 1987–2003* [Internet]. Available from <http://www.btselem.org/English/Statistics/Total_Casualties.asp> [Accessed 6 September 2003]

—— (2003b) *Fatalities in the al-Aqsa Intifada, Data by Month* [Internet]. Available from <http://www.btselem.org/English/Statistics/Al_Aqsa_Fatalities_Tables.asp> [Accessed 6 September 2003]

—— (2003c) *Behind the Barrier: Human Rights Violation as a Result of Israel's Separation Barrier.* B'Tselem Position Paper, April

—— (2000) *Illusions of Restraint* Report, December

Cattan, H. (1973) *Palestine and International Law* (London: Longman)

Childers, E. (1976) 'The Wordless Wish: From Citizens to Refugees', in *The Palestinian Issue in Middle East Peace Efforts*, hearings before the Committee on International Relations, House of Representatives, September, October, November 1975 (US Government Printing Office)

Chomsky, N. (1999) *The Fateful Triangle: The United States, Israel and the Palestinians* (London: Pluto Press)

—— (1992) *Deterring Democracy* (London: Vintage Books)

Cockburn, A. & Cockburn, L. (1991) *Dangerous Liaison: The Inside Story of the US–Israeli Covert Relationship* (New York: HarperCollins)

Cohn-Sherbok, D. (2001) 'A Jewish Perspective', in D. Cohn-Sherbok and D. El-Alami (eds), *The Palestine–Israeli Conflict: A Beginner's Guide* (Oxford: One World Publications)

Crum, B.C. (1947) *Behind the Silken Curtain* (New York: Simon & Schuster)

Dodd, P. and Barakat, H. (1968) *Rivers Without Bridges* (Beirut: Institute for Palestine Studies)

Eban, A. (1992) *Personal Witness: Israel through My Eyes* (New York: Putnam Publishing)

—— (1977) *An Autobiography* (New York: Random House)

Eddy, W. (1954) *F.D.R. Meets Ibn Saud* (New York: American Friends of the Middle East)

Feingold, H.L. (1970) *The Politics of Rescue* (New Brunswick: Rutgers University Press)

Finkelstein, N.G. (2001) *Image and Reality of the Israel–Palestine Conflict* (London: Verso)

—— (1996) *The Rise and Fall of Palestine: A Personal Account of the Intifada Years* (Minneapolis: University of Minnesota Press)

Fisch, H. (1982) *The Zionism of Zion* (in Hebrew) (Tel-Aviv: Zmora Bitan)

Fisk, R. (2001) *Pity the Nation* (Oxford: Oxford University Press)

Flapan, S. (1987) *The Birth of Israel: Myths and Realities* (New York: Pantheon Books)

Foundation for Middle East Peace (1997) *Settler Population 1972–97* [Internet]. Available from: <http://www.fmep.org/charts/chart9811_1.gif> [Accessed 6 September 2003]

Friedlander, D. & Goldscheider, C. (1979) *The Population of Israel* (New York: Columbia University Press)

Gabbay, R. (1959) *A Political Study of the Arab–Jewish Conflict: the Arab Refugee Problem* (Geneva: Librairie E. Droz)

Gilbert, M. (1999) *Israel: A History* (London: Black Swan Books)

Gush Shalom (2003) *Barak's Generous Offers* [Internet]. Available from: <http://www.gush-shalom.org/generous/generous.html> [Accessed 6 September 2003]

—— (1998) *Who is Violating the Agreements?* [Internet]. Available from: <http://www.gush-shalom.org/archives/oslo.html> [Accessed 6 September 2003]

Harris, W.W. (1980) *Taking Root: Israeli Settlement in the West Bank, the Golan and Gaza–Sinai 1967–1980* (Chichester: Research Studies Press)

Heller, Y. (1985) *The Struggle for the State: Zionist Diplomacy of the years 1936–48* [Hebrew] (Jerusalem: Jewish Agency Protocols)

Herzl, T. (1960) *The Complete Diaries of Theodor Herzl* (New York: Herzl Press and Thomas Yoseloff)

Hirst, D. (1977) *The Gun and the Olive Branch* (London: Faber & Faber)

Hitchens, C. & Said, E. (1988) *Blaming the Victims* (London: Verso)

Human Rights Watch (1999) 'Israel/Lebanon, Persona Non Grata: The Expulsion of Civilians from Israeli-Occupied Lebanon' [Internet]. Available from: <http://hrw.org/reports/1999/lebanon/Isrlb997.htm> [Accessed 13 January 2004]

—— (1998) *Security Pact May Encourage Human Rights Violations*. Press Release, New York, 22 October 1998

—— (1996) *Israel's Closure of the West Bank and Gaza Strip*, July 1996, vol. 8, no. 3 (E)

Hunter, J. (1996) *Israeli Foreign Policy: South Africa and Central America* (Boston: South End Press)

Independent Television Commission (2003) *The Public's View*, 33 Foley Street, London W1 W7

Ingrams, D. (1972) *Palestine Papers 1917–1922, Seeds of Conflict* (London: John Murray)

Israeli Defence Force (2003) *Israeli Civilians Killed/Wounded on the Lebanese Border 1985–99* [Internet]. Available from: <http://www.idf.il/english/statistics/civilian.stm> [Accessed 5 September 2003]

Israeli Ministry of Foreign Affairs (2004) *The Cabinet Resolution Regarding the Disengagement Plan*, 6 June 2004 [Internet]. Available from: <http://www.mfa.gov.il/MFA/Peace+Process/Reference+Documents/Revised+Disengagement+Plan+6-June-2004.htm> [Accessed 5 February 2006]

—— (1999) *Suicide and Other Bombing Attacks Inside Israel Since the Declaration of Principles, September 1993* [Internet]. Available from: <http://www.mfa.gov.il/mfa/go.asp?MFAH0i5d0> [Accessed 5 September 2003]

—— (1996) *Israel's Settlements: Their Conformity with International Law* [Internet]. Available from: <http://www.israel.org/mfa/go.asp?MFAH0dgj0> [Accessed 5 September 2003]

Kapeliouk, A. (1984) *Sabra and Shatila: Inquiry into a Massacre* (Belmont, MA: Association of Arab-American University Graduates)

Karsh, E. (2000) *Fabricating Israeli History: The 'New Historians'* (London: Frank Cass)

Khalidi, W. (1988) 'Plan Dalet: Master Plan for the Conquest of Palestine', *Journal of Palestine Studies*, Autumn 1988

Kimmerling (1983) *Zionism & Territory: The Socio-Territorial Dimension of Zionist Politics* (Berkeley: University of California Press)

Laqueur, W. & Rubin, B. (1984) *The Israel–Arab Reader* (New York: Facts on File/Viking Penguin)

Lilienthal, A. (1978) *The Zionist Connection* (New York: Dodd, Mead & Co.)

Linowitz, S. (1957) 'The Legal Basis for the State of Israel', *American Bar Association Journal*, vol. 43

Lorch, N. (1961) *The Edge of the Sword: Israel's War of Independence, 1947–1949* (New York: Putnam)

Lustick, I. (1980) *Arabs in the Jewish State: Israel's Control of a National Minority* (New York: University of Texas Press)

McCarthy, J. (1990) *The Population of Palestine* (New York: Columbia University Press)

Masalha, N. (1999) 'The 1967 Palestinian Exodus', in G. Karmi and E. Cotran (eds), *The Palestinian Exodus 1948–1998* (London: Garnet Publishing)

—— (1992) *Expulsion of the Palestinians: The Concept of 'Transfer' in Zionist Political Thought* (Beirut: Institute for Palestine Studies)

Mayhew, C. (1973) *Crossroads to Israel* (Bloomington: Indiana University Press)

Mishal, S. & Sela, A. (2000) *The Palestinian Hamas: Vision, Violence and Coexistence* (New York: Columbia University Press)

Morris, B. (2001) *Righteous Victims: A History of the Zionist–Arab Conflict* (New York: Vintage Books)

—— (1997) *Israel's Border Wars, 1949–1956: Arab Infiltration, Israeli Retaliation, and the Countdown to the Suez War* (Oxford: Oxford University Press)

—— (1992) *Israel's Secret Wars: A History of Israel's Intelligence Services* (London: Futura Publications)

—— (1989) *The Birth of the Palestinian Refugee Problem* (London: Cambridge University Press)

Neff, D. (1985) *Warriors for Jerusalem* (New York: Smithmark Publishing)

Netanyahu, B. (2000) *A Durable Peace: Israel and its Place Among the Nations* (New York: Warner Books)

Ovendale, R. (1999) *The Origins of the Arab–Israeli Wars* (Harlow: Pearson)

Pappe, I. (1999) 'Were they Expelled? The History, Historiography and Relevance of the Palestinian Refugee Problem', in G. Karmi and E. Cotran (eds), *The Palestinian Exodus 1948–1998* (Reading: Garnet Publishing)

Perlmutter, A., Handel, M. and Bar-Joseph, U. (1982) *Two Minutes over Baghdad* (London: Vallentine Mitchell)

Peters, J. (1984) *From Time Immemorial: The Origins of the Arab–Jewish Conflict over Palestine* (New York: HarperCollins)

Philo, G. (2002) 'Television News and Audience Understanding of War, Conflict and Disaster', *Journalism Studies*, vol. 3, no.2 (London: Routledge)

Pundak, R. (2001) 'From Oslo to Taba: What Went Wrong?' *Survival*, vol. 43, no. 3

Randal, J. (1983) *The Tragedy of Lebanon: Christian Warlords, Israeli Adventurers and American Bunglers* (London: Chatto & Windus/ Hogarth Press)

Rusk, D. (1992) *As I Saw It* (New York: Penguin USA)

Sachar, H.M. (1977) *A History of Israel: From the Rise of Zionism to Our Time* (Oxford: Blackwell)

Segev, T. (2001) *One Palestine, Complete. Jews and Arabs Under the British Mandate* (London: Abacus)

—— (1993) *The Seventh Million: The Israelis and the Holocaust* (New York: Hill & Wang)

Shafir, G. (1999) 'Zionism and Colonialism', in I. Pappe (ed.), *The Israel/Palestine Question* (New York: Routledge)

Shahak, I. (1995) *Analysis of Israeli Policies: The Priority of the Ideological Factor*. Report 154. 12 May

Shahak, I. & Mezvinsky, N. (1999) *Jewish Fundamentalism in Israel* (London: Pluto Press)

Shlaim, A. (2003) 'The War of the Israeli Historians'. Talk given at Georgetown University, 1 December [Internet]. Available from:

<http://ccas.georgetown.edu/research-pubs.cfm?cid=96&ctype=1> [Accessed 11 June 2006]

—— (2000) *The Iron Wall: Israel and the Arab World* (London: Penguin)

Shonfeld, M. (1977) *The Holocaust Victims Accuse: Documents and Testimony on Jewish War Criminals, Part I* (Brooklyn: Neturei Karta of USA)

Tillman, S. (1982) *The United States in the Middle East: Interests and Obstacles* (Bloomington: University of Indiana Press)

United Nations (1999) Commission on Human Rights. 'Question of the Violation of Human Rights in the Occupied Arab Territories, Including Palestine'. E/CN.4/RES/1999/5, 23 April

—— (1997) 'Illegal Israeli actions in Occupied East Jerusalem and the Rest of the Occupied Palestinian Territory'. Resolution A/RES/ES-10/2, passed 25 April

—— (1996) 'UN Report on Israel's Bombing of the United Nations Compound at Qana, Lebanon'. S1996/337, 7 May

—— (1994) Commission on Human Rights. 'Question of the Violation of Human Rights in the Occupied Arab Territories, Including Palestine'. E/CN.4/RES/1994/3 (A+B)E/1994/24E/CN.4/1994/132, 18 February

—— (1990) 'The Origins and Evolution of the Palestine Problem 1917–1988' [Internet]. Available from: <http://domino.un.org/UNISPAL.NSF/561c6ee353d740fb8525607d00581829/aeac80e740c782e4852561150071fdb0!OpenDocument> [Accessed 6 September 2003]

—— (1988) 'Report of the Special Committee to Investigate Israeli Practices Affecting the Human Rights of the Population of the Occupied Territories'. Resolution 43/58A, passed 6 December

—— (1967) General Assembly, Fifth Emergency Session, 5 July

—— (1945) League of Nations. 'The Mandate System. Origin Applications Principles'. 30 April 1985. LoN/1945, VI.A.1

Usher, G. (2006) 'The Wall and the Dismemberment of Palestine', *Race & Class*, vol. 47, pp. 9–30

Weisgal, M. (1944) *Chaim Weizmann* (New York: Dial Press)

Yisraeli, D. (1974) *The Palestine Problem in German Politics* (Bar Ilan University: Ramat Gan)

Index

Compiled by Sue Carlton

Printed in Great Britain
by Amazon